D1742712

STOP ANXIETY IN RELATIONSHIP

How to Understand Couple Conflicts to Eliminate Jealousy and Insecurity in Your Relationships! Stop Negative Thinking, Attachment and Fear of Abandonment, Improve Communication

By

LEROY REYNOLDS

TABLE OF CONTENTS

5

This report is designed to provide precise and solid information on the issue and issue secured. The supply is marketed with the alternative of not allowing the manufacturer to make book-keeping, officially approved administrations or anything else. If an exhortation is important, legitimate or competent, a rehearsed person in the call should be requested.

The Statement of Values, which was also accepted and approved by the American Bar Association Commission and the Publications & Associations Panel.

It is not permissible to replicate copy or transmit any part of this report in any electronic method or group. Authorization of this delivery is carefully disallowed, and the report's ability is not allowed unless the seller has written the approval. All ownership. All rights held.

The data provided herein is conveyed, to be truthful and consistent in that the beneficiary's clear and articulate duty is any danger, in so far as absence of attitude or otherwise, through any use or misuse of any methods, procedures or belongings inside them. Any legal obligation or liability will be kept against the seller for any reparation, damage or financial misfortune because of the results, either clearly or inferred.

All copyrights not held by the distributor are claimed by particular creators.

The statistics in this paper are primarily for educational purposes and are all-inclusive. The data are entered without a contract or any confirmation of assurance.

The trademarks used are without consent and the trademark distribution is without the consent or support of the trademark owner. Both trademarks and trademarks in the book are solely for the purpose of illustrating and are clearly managed and not associated by the founders.

INTRODUCTION

Relationships can be one of the planet's most rewarding experiences, but they can also be a fertile ground for negative thoughts and emotions.

Anxiety regarding relationships can occur at nearly any stage of courtship. Only thinking about being in a relationship will bring up stress for many single people. When and when people begin dating, the early stages will present them with constant worries: "Does he/she really like me?" "Will this work out?" "How serious is this?" Sadly, in the later stages of a romantic union, these worries do not appear to subside. Indeed, as things get closer to a couple, anxiety can become even more severe. "Is this last one?" "Do I really like him/her?" "Do we have to slow down?" "Am I really ready for this kind of commitment?" "Will he/she lose interest?" All this thinking about our relationships is making us feel pretty lonely. It could give us reason to separate ourselves from our partners. Our fear at its worst can even lead us to give up on love altogether. Knowing more about the cause and effect of the anxieties of relationships will help us to recognize negative thoughts and patterns which can undermine our love lives. Why do we suppress our impulses and become vulnerable to those we love?

Anxiety is one of the most prominent nosological agents not only encountered in psychiatry but also in general practice. Janet described this as "fear without substance."

Anxiety, anxiety, anxiety, fear, fear, fear, agony, panic — It's a long list of synonyms!

Very fine differences between these notions can often lead to confusion: it is normal to feel perplexed, but is it all right to be anxious? If that's the case, then usual anxiety is present. What's anguishing? Can we, on the other hand, live without worries?

Anxiety disorders are amongst the world's most severe psychological disorders. Until the 1980s, generalized anxiety disorder (GAD) was known as 'anxiety neurosis.' Anxiety disorders contain various forms of extreme and dangerous anxiety and anxiety. Existing medical diagnosis guidelines classify a wide number of anxiety disorders. Psychological disorders are generally very prevalent among adults and particularly adults with chronic illnesses.

Many types of anxiety can be observed: epidemiological and genetic causes, biological origins, cognitive psychology, emotional and physical comorbidity, tolerance to medication, biochemical and animal research, experimental and behavioral types. Advances in drug discovery and psychosocial treatment approaches have been made, but many patients remain symptomatic.

General Anxiety Disorder, which falls within the category of anxiety disorders with symptoms of anxiety, worry, and apparent alertness, has a fairly constant prevalence (5-6.5 percent) in the general population.

Anxiety patients often consult primary care physicians for their treatment, but in most cases, do not accept the diagnosis of anxiety disorder. Diagnosis of anxiety disorder could result in a longer period of hospitalization, more frequent use of diagnostic tests and medication, and, therefore, a high financial burden. This reduces the quality of life and causes serious family problems and a prolonged absence from work.

Anxiety is a symptom that can be found in many endogenous conditions and can be associated with almost any medical illness. Anxiety disorders are normal and are related to extreme anxiety and dysfunction. There are complex dominant signs, but they include constant nervousness, trembling, muscle stiffness, sweating, lightheadedness, palpitations, dizziness, and epigastric pain. Anxiety disorders represent a disability and social disability as serious as chronic somatic disorders such as arthritis, hypertension, asthma, or diabetes. Stigmatization is an important factor in the inadequacy of diagnosis, which can account for why a significant number of patients do not express emotional problems to their physicians.

The relationship between anxiety and the cardiovascular system has been known since the 19th century. We often say, when we have anxieties, that it is a heartache, and we often use the term "broken heart" after a severe pain or an anxious period.

In everyday medical practice, co-morbidity and consecutive anxiety disorders can be seen in patients with moderate to high osteoarthritis, which is a painful disabling joint disease. In our everyday life, eating is a very important thing, not only to support our body, but we may enjoy every meal. Food disorders could also be dangerous. Obesity is now one of the world's greatest public health issues. There is a link between anxiety disorders and obesity. Obesity is considered to be a modern illness. It seems that it is spreading rapidly throughout the world, just like anxiety. Eating disorders, such as anorexia and bulimia, could be linked not only to fashion models but also to psychiatric disorders, such as anxiety.

Study over the past 20 years has shown that epilepsy patients also have coexisting psychiatric issues, including mood problems, anxiety problems, and psychotic problems.

The balance system is often disrupted. Patients with anxiety often say, "I've lost my balance." A frequent question in neurotological expertise is whether the dizziness of psychiatric patients with anxiety disorders is caused by vestibular dysfunction, or whether the dizziness is caused by psychiatric disorders. A high level of psychiatric disorders has been repeatedly described among patients with organic vertiginous syndromes and has been attributed to vestibular dysfunction. Differential diagnosis can only be achieved by a careful interdisciplinary way of thinking and activity, given that vestibular, neurological, and psychiatric disorders – considered pathogenic factors – are present at the same time when symptoms are triggered, and overlaps can occur between certain pathological processes.

So, we can see that anxiety problems also cover all areas of our life in the medical and daily senses.

Simply put, falling in love scares us in ways we don't expect. The more we trust another, the more we are to lose. We are afraid of getting hurt in several ways, both conscious and unconscious. To a certain degree, we all have a fear of being close. Interestingly, this anxiety always shows up when we get exactly what we want when we experience love like we never have or are handled in different ways.

When we move into a partnership, it's not just the things that happen between us and our partner that make us anxious; it's the stuff about what's going on that we say ourselves. The "powerful inner voice" is a phrase used to describe the mean coach we all have in our heads who criticizes us, imposes bad advice on us and fuel our fear of intimacy. "You're never going to find someone, so why even try?" "You can't trust him. He's searching for anyone better." "She doesn't really love you. Get out before you get hurt." This cynical inner voice makes us turn against ourselves and the people around us. This can encourage aggressive, pessimistic, and suspicious thinking that reduces our self-esteem and induces unhealthy levels of mistrust, defensiveness, envy, and anxiety. In fact, it feeds a steady stream of thoughts that ruins our satisfaction and makes us worry about our relationship, rather than just enjoy it.

Once we get into our minds, dwelling on those worrying feelings, we get extremely disconnected from our partner's actual relationship. We may begin to behave in negative ways, to make nasty comments, or to become immature or authoritarian towards our significant others. Imagine your partner staying at work late in one night, for instance. Sitting alone at home, your inner critic starts to tell you, "Where is she? Can you really trust her? She probably wants to stay away from you. She's trying to hide you. She doesn't even love you anymore." These thoughts will snowball in your mind until you feel nervous, angry, or suspicious when your partner gets home. You can be behaving angry or cold, then set off your partner to feel irritated and defensive. Eventually, you changed the dynamic between yourself completely. Instead of enjoying the time you have with each other, you may be wasting a whole night feeling disconnected and upset. Now the gap you originally expected was essentially forced. The culprit behind this prophecy, which fulfills itself, is not the situation itself. It's that vital inner voice that warped your thought, skewed your perceptions, and eventually led you down a destructive path.

When it comes to all the issues that we worry about in relationships, we're far more resilient than we think. In reality, we're able to deal with the hurts and rejections we fear so much. We will feel pain, and eventually heal. The vital inner voice, however, appears to terrorize and disastrously affect reality. It can stir up severe anxiety spells about non-existent complexities and risks that are not even observable. Even if real things happen, someone breaks up with us or has an interest in somebody else; our vital inner voice will tear us apart in ways that we don't deserve. It will distort reality absolutely, and weaken our power and resilience. The pessimistic roommate is the one who always gives poor advice. "You can't survive this. Just put up your guard and never be vulnerable to someone else." Our particular perceptions and adaptations depend on the defenses we develop and the vital voices we hear. Some of us tend to be clinging and aggressive in our actions when we feel nervous or uncertain.

In response, we may feel possessive or controlling towards our partner. Conversely, some of us in our relationships can feel easily intruded upon. We may withdraw from our partners; separate ourselves from our desire feelings. We may behave aloof, distant, or guarded. Such related trends may come from our early styles of attachment. The pattern of attachment is formed in the attachments to the childhood and continues to serve as a working model for adult relationships. This affects how every one of us is reacting to our needs and how we are going to fulfill them. Various types of attachment can cause us to experience different degrees of anxiety about relationships.

The unique critical inner voices that we have about ourselves, our spouses, and relationships are developed by the early behaviors to which we have been exposed in our families or in society at large.

Cultural assumptions, as well as behaviors our powerful caretakers have about themselves and others, will invade our perspective and shade our current perceptions. Although the inner critic of everything is different, some that critical inner voices include:

Negative Inner Voices about the Relationship

Humans just end up getting hurt.

Nor will marriages work out.

Voices are so dismissive about your partner people

Women are so delicate, so weak, and so indirect.

He only wants to be with friends of his.

Why get so excited? What's so sweet of her anyway?

Perhaps, he cheats on you.

You can't believe her.

He really can't get it right.

Voices concerning Yourself

You'll never find anyone else who knows you.

Don't get too hooked on her.

He doesn't care about you, really.

She's perfect for you too.

You have to maintain an interest in him.

You're better off alone.

She will ignore you until she gets to know you.

You have to be in charge of this.

When he gets angry, then it's your fault.

Don't be too weak, or actually get hurt.

CHAPTER 3 - HOW DOES ANXIETY AFFECT US IN RELATIONSHIPS?

As we shed light on our history, we quickly realize that there are many early factors that influenced our pattern of attachment, our psychological defenses, and our vital voice inside.

All of these factors contribute to our insecurity about relationships and can, in many ways, lead us to sabotage our lives of love. Hearing our inner critic and giving in to this anxiety will lead to the following actions:

Cling – Our propensity to be violent towards our partner when we are nervous. Once we entered the relationship, we may stop feeling like the independent, powerful people we were. As a consequence, we can easily fall apart, behave jealously or dangerously, or no longer participate in independent activities.

Control-We can try to overpower or influence our partner when we feel threatened. We can lay down rules on what they can and can't do just to relieve our own feelings of fear or anxiety. This action can alienate our partner and make us feel resentful.

Reject – When we are uncertain about our relationship, it is aloofness that is one of the defenses we can turn to. To defend ourselves or to beat our partner to the punch, we might become cold or refuse. Such acts can be subtle or explicit, but in our partner, it is almost always a sure way to cause distance or build fear.

Withhold – Often, we prefer to withhold from our partner when we feel nervous or afraid, as opposed to overt rejection. Perhaps things got close, and we feel agitated, so we withdraw. We hold back tiny affections or give up on some aspect of our relationship entirely. To withhold may seem like a passive act, but it's one of the quietest killers of desire and attraction in a relationship.

Punish – Our reaction to our distress is often more violent, and we are simply punishing, taking our feelings out on our partner. We can shout and scream, or give the cold shoulder to our partner. It is essential to know about how much our activities are a reaction to our accomplice and the amount they are a solution to our fundamental voice inside.

Withdraw – We may give up real acts of love and intimacy when we feel scared in a relationship and withdraw into a "fantasy bond." A fantasy bond is an illusion of attachment that replaces real acts of love. In this fantasy state, we focus on shape over substance. We can stay in the relationship to feel secure but give up on the important parts of the relationship. In a bond of illusion, we frequently indulge in many of the above described detrimental behaviors as a way of creating distance and protecting ourselves against the insecurity that inevitably comes with feeling safe and in love. Learn more about the bond between fantasies here.

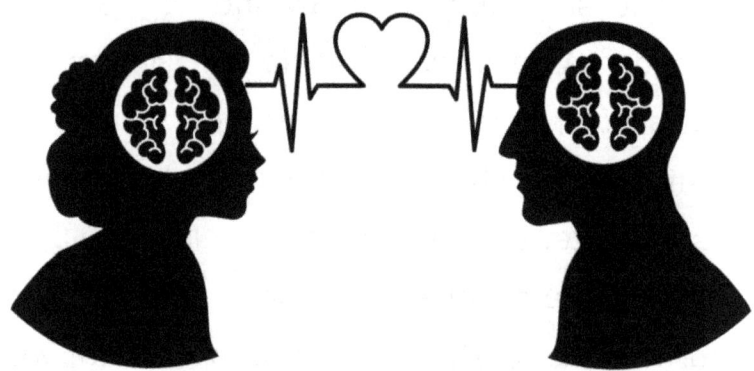

Intimate relationships are a mirror that represents the best and worst of us all. They can inflame or soothe our struggles. They can feel like sorcery when they're right.

Even when they are exactly right, anxiety will steal the magic and loosen the bond between two individuals who belong together. All relationships call for trust, tenderness, flexibility, and vulnerability. People with anxiety also have these by the truckload and will give the partnership generously. The problem is that, often, anxiety will erode them almost as easily.

If you're someone dealing with anxiety, there's plenty of stuff about you that will make you easy to love. All relationships often struggle, and the difficulties can be very common – quite natural, and precise when anxiety is at play.

Anxiety can function in interesting ways, and it can have different impacts on different relationships, and not all of the following will apply to each relation. Here are some ways to improve and secure your relationship from the effects of anxiety:

Top up the emotional capital

You are likely to be extremely sensitive to the needs of others and offer your relationship freely and abundantly. However, anxiety can also drain the resources out of the relationship almost as quickly as you spend them. That's all right – there's plenty of good that comes with loving you to make up for this – but it may mean you've got to keep making sure that those benefits are balanced. Heap your partner with love, appreciation, affection, touch-loads of touch-and talk around him or her whenever you can.

Let your partner also see you as a support

Your partner may feel reluctant to 'burden' you with worries, particularly if those worries do not seem as big as those with which you are struggling. People with anxiety have too much energy – without it, it is difficult to cope with anxiety – and make sure your partner knows it doesn't matter how big or small their challenges are, sometimes you can be the strong one too. The inclination may be for anxious people's spouses to throw off their fears, but that may mean they take themselves out of the ability to feel nurtured and protected by you – which would be a great loss for both of you. Often be careful in being the rock too. Ask, hold on, press. Nothing is more relieving than the solace of the individual you love.

Let your partner in on whatever you think

Anxious thoughts are supremely personal, but let them in on your partner. It is a big part of intimacy. Often, you'll talk about what you need to do to feel safe, what it feels bad for you, and what could go wrong. You'll also have a great capacity to think about other people — anxious people do — but make sure you let the feelings that detain you join in. Holding stuff to yourself so much has a tendency to expand the gap between two men.

It's perfectly fine to ask for reassurance-just not too much

Anxiety has a way to creep through it all. It can make you question the stuff that doesn't deserve to be questioned when it's left unchecked – such as your connection. Asking your partner for reassurance is absolutely alright and very natural. Everything the same, too much, and it could be felt as neediness. Neediness is the enemy of desire and can smother the flame over time. Make sure your partner has the chance to naturally love you, without asking you – it's good for them and much better for you.

Place yourself open

The fear may have various effects on relationships. It could stoke the need for constant reassurance in some people. It may cause them to hold back in others, lessening their susceptibility to a heart attack. Vulnerability is beautiful – being vulnerable to another – and it is the core of good, stable relationships. The problem with over-protecting yourself is that it may encourage the very rejection you're trying to avoid. Part of intimacy is to bring someone in deeper than the rest of the world. It's trusting the person with your delicate, messy, untamed bits – the bits that are always amazing, often baffling, and fine with the person who loves you. It's normal to worry about what could happen if someone has open access to these parts of you, but see those concerns as what they are – fears, not facts – and trust that whatever happens when you open up to love and care, you're going to be all right since you are going to be.

Be aware that anxiety is creeping into your relationship

Especially nothing can cause anxiety – that's one of the terrible things about it – so it's going to look for a goal, an anchor to hold it still and make sense. When you're in an intimate relationship, the bulls' eye will sit here, pulling your fear into their gravitational pull. This can create suspicions, envy, distrust, and insecurity. Anxiety can be such a scoundrel. That doesn't mean that your relationship deserves your anxiety – most likely it doesn't – but it's significant, real, and always in your thoughts, making it a very simple goal. Remind yourself that this doesn't mean there is anything to think about just because you're concerned. If you have to worry, but then see it for what it is – fear and not reality. You're happy, you're nervous, and you're good. Let the truth hold you up.

Analysis causes paralysis

There is a saying-' Thinking is leading to paralysis, 'and it does. 'Is it charity? Or fanfare? Or am I being kidding myself? What if my heart splits into tiny bits of jagged material? However, can it work if we don't want the same music/books/food/films? What if we're booking a holiday and the airline is going on strike? What if we get sick? And what if we both get sick? What if we will not be able to get a refund? Or does the mortgage pay? What if it makes me sick? 'Yeah. I assume you know what that sounds like. What you're focused on is what becomes important, because if you concentrate on the potential issues, they'll drain your attention until they're large enough to cause trouble themselves. They're going to rob your strength, the sense of fun, and the ability to move. You probably know this already, but what to do about it. Try something here ... Set a timeline in which you can act as if things are going to be perfect. So, for instance, worry every day from 10-3 and then relax, let go and behave as if things are going to be perfect. You're not expected to believe it – just 'act as if.' Tomorrow, you will have another opportunity to think if you need to. Be driven by the facts and not by the doubts that torment you at 2 am.

Close up. No. No. Go. Go

The stuff can get wobbly when you concentrate on every aspect. You concentrate on things that aren't right with your partner or your relationship while simultaneously seeking reassurance that your significant other loves you and is committed to it. This can cause you to drive away your partner ('You've disappointed me,') and then pull him or her close ('Tell me you love me. You love me, right?'). Have a chat with your partner and set up a secure way for your partner to find out when it is happening, whether it is a common procedure. Agree on what they look like. When it happens, be careful not to hear it as a criticism – it's not – in the way you love each other, it is your partner looking for some peace.

The rough talk will get you stronger

All relationships now and then have to deal with the tough stuff, but anxiety can make things more stressful and bigger than they are. The tendency may be to avoid talking to your partner about difficult things, due to worries about what the partnership could bring. Difficult things don't go anywhere-they're festering until they melt. Trust your partner – and you – can cope with a difficult debate. Relationships are founded on confidence, and it is an important one to the confidence that your partnership will power through hard conversations.

In what it is like to be, you let your partner in

We, humans, are dynamic creatures, and having someone closer to you is the lifeblood of love and your story – even if it's someone who has been with you for a while. Individuals change, stories change, and it's easy to lose contact with the person who sleeps next to at nighttime, even in intimate relationships. In what your fear is about, you let your partner in. Talk about your feelings, how you are influenced by anxiety, job, friendship, family, and how grateful you are for love and support.

Let the partner know what's causing you

Is there a particular circumstance that appears to shed light on your anxiety?

Massive crowds? Fremdlers? Exit Hardships? Loud music inside your car? Is he late? Speak to your partner so that if you unwontedly find yourself in the situation, he or she can understand what is happening.

You might be tempted to push for a fast answer to a problem or issue within your relationship, as a way to feel better and relieve your anxiety.

You may become frustrated with the willingness of your partner to hold or put off committing to a course of action, or their resistance to continuing to speak about the issue, however, be sensitive to the possibility that your partner can see things differently, even more clearly. Breathe, chat, and don't presume that your partner takes time or pulls out of the discussion due to lack of commitment, or that the problem isn't enough.

Verify that you are looking after yourself

Falling in love is crazy sweet, but taking care of yourself and caring for your special one will take your focus away. We all appear to do this, but it can be especially troublesome for people with anxiety as the ripple has undone certain things if you're off-balance. So, you need to take good care of yourself. Eating well (a healthy, omega-3-rich diet, low in carbohydrates and sugars), and physical exercise and meditation will help protect the brain from anxiety. If you feel insecure about yourself, think about it this way: it's not really nice to expect your partner to support you through your anxiety if you don't do anything to support yourself. Think of self-care as investing in you, your family, and friendship. Remember that anxiety is good for everybody, so talk to your partner about following a healthy lifestyle together – eating, exercising, and meditating together.

Understand that your partner would need boundaries

Creating boundaries can be a positive thing for the partnership to remain together, safe, and linked. Understand that limits are not the reason your partner locks you out but as a means of self-protecting your anxiety from 'keeping up.' You may be stressed and need to speak over and over about it, but that's not really what's going to be good for you, your partner, or your relationship. Your partner will love you, drawing a strong heavy focus between the last time you talk about it and the next time you want to. It's easy to chat, but talking over and over about the same thing will drain and create a problem when no one has. Know that your partners love you and that limits are necessary to foster love and create relationships and not to oppose them. Speak to your partner about what he or she wants in the face of your distress to feel better. Invite the limits – it will help keep your relationship healthy and caring and make your partner feel as though he or she can retain a sense of self without being overwhelmed by your concerns. Anxiety is infectious, and if your partner decides to draw a line (in the end) around your anxiety, let it happen – it will help maintain the relationship's emotional capital and will be beneficial for both of you.

Laugh and joke

That's just so necessary! Laughter is a natural solution to the anxiety-inducing stress and tension. Laughing together will deepen the bond between you, and when there's been a rough couple of days (weeks? months?), it'll help both of you remember why you fell in love with one another. Anxiety has a way to make you forget that life wasn't always meant to be taken seriously. If your partner sees you laugh (who will be lovely and undoubtedly one of the reasons he or she fell for you for the first time), you have to find a justification-a funny video, memories, YouTube ... There's something.

The fall in love is supposed to bc beautiful, but to get close to another person at the best of times is not without its peaks and lows. Intimacy is a conduit for every possible emotion, from the joy of knowing that someone very wonderful is as moved by you as you are by them, to the anguish of self-doubt and potential loss, to the comfort, richness and sometimes stillness of a deeper love. Anxiety affects relationships, but you can protect your relationship and make it one that is solid, close, and resilient by being open to its effect and actively reacting to it.

CHAPTER 6 - HOW TO ELIMINATE JEALOUSY AND INSECURITY IN YOUR RELATIONSHIP

J
E
A
L
O
U
S
Y

Overcoming envy is like altering every mental or behavioral reaction. It begins with knowledge. Knowledge lets you see that the stories that are projected in your mind are not real. You no longer respond when you have this insight into the scenarios that your mind imagines.

Jealousy and anger are emotional responses that are not true in believing situations in your head. In modifying what you think, you change what your mind is creating, so you will remove these emotional damaging reactions. Even when the reaction is warranted, envy and frustration aren't helpful ways to cope with the situation and get what we want. When you're in the emotion, trying to alter rage or jealousy is like trying to stop a car skidding on ice. If you can steer clear of the danger until we get there, your ability to manage the situation is greatly enhanced. It means confronting certain biases that cause envy rather than attempting to suppress your emotions.

Dissolving the feelings like rage and envy in relationships completely means shifting the core values of fear and unconscious expectations of what your partner is doing.

There are a number of elements that establish the jealousy dynamics. As such, sustainable approaches would have to tackle various elements of values, opinions, desires, and the strength of a person would. If you ignore one or more of these components, then you leave the door open to return to those negative emotions and behaviors.

You can step back from the story by doing a few basic exercises, which project your mind and refrain from the emotional reaction. If you just want to change your feelings and behavior, only you should do it. Learning valuable skills takes only desire. In the Self Mastery Courses, you'll find useful exercises and activities to conquer the emotional envy reaction.

Principle envy causes are assumptions that cause feelings of insecurity

Feelings of low self-esteem are centered on perceptions that we have in a mental picture of who we are. We don't have to change to remove the fear and low self-esteem; we only have to change our confidence in the false self-image. While some may believe that this may be difficult, it is only daunting because most may not have developed the requisite skills to alter a belief. When you learn the skills, you find it takes very little time to alter a belief. You just stop trusting yourself in the plot. It takes more time to believe it than not to believe it.

Self-judgment will intensify the sense of vulnerability

It is not enough to scientifically "learn" that we generate the emotion. With only this detail, it is likely that the Inner Judge will harass us with criticism for what we do. The

Inner Judge could use this knowledge to bring us into more vulnerability on an emotional downward spiral. You will need to develop skills to remove the religions and distorted self-images and take ownership of what your mind ideas are for real positive change.

One of the steps to alter behavior is to see how the pictures, values, and perceptions actually create the emotion of rage or envy in our minds. This step not only encourages us to take responsibility but also places us in a position of power to change our emotions.

If you're in a jealous partner relationship and they want you to change your behavior in order to escape envy, then they don't take responsibility. When they say something like, "If you wouldn't, then I wouldn't respond like this." That kind of language signals an attitude of powerlessness and an effort to manipulate your actions through a deal.

How the mind produces the feelings of jealousy and anger

I discussed in the description below on the mechanisms of jealousy and anger. If you're trying to overcome envy, you probably already know the complexities I'm explaining. This explanation can help fill some holes in how the mind twists awareness into the judgment of itself and reinforces low self-esteem and insecurity. This intellectual understanding can help to build awareness to see these dynamics as you do them. But you will need a different set of skills to really make effective changes. Knowing how to create your emotional reactions does not provide you with sufficient information on how to change them. Much like realizing that you have a flat tire because you've been driving over a nail doesn't mean you know how to fix the tyre.

I am going to use a guy as the jealous partner for the illustration. I'm referring to various pictures in your mind, and you can use the diagram below as a reference. This starts with a man who feels uncertain about himself. Insecurity stems from his "not good enough" False Hidden Picture. The man induces self-rejection in his mind with the idea that this fake image is him rather than a picture in his mind. The mental consequence of self-rejection is a feeling of indignity, discomfort, apprehension, and unhappiness.

Compensating for insecurity

He is relying on his perceived positive attributes in order to alleviate the emotion created by his Hidden False Image. The human produces a more optimistic False

Picture of himself from these attributes. I call this the Picture Projected because that's how he wants to be seen. The emotional result of a good self-image is no self-rejection and no feeling of indignity. There is greater self-acceptance, and he generates more love and joy. Note he hasn't shifted, he's just holding on to a different picture depending on the moment in his mind.

The expectations of the Secret Image are the causes of unhappiness, while the Projected Image causes more positive feelings. Please note that both photos are fake. Both pictures are in the imagination of the man, and neither is he. He is the one who, in his imagination, produces and responds to the pictures. He is not an imaginary image.

The mind of the man is drawn to associate the Projected Image with the characteristics of women. The attributes are also seen as good because of the fact that women are drawn to them. When a man gets attention from the woman, instead of the "Not Good Enough" image, he associates himself with the Predicted Image. In his emotional state, the increased confidence in the Predicted Picture results in more self-acceptance, affection, and satisfaction.

It is the acceptance and loving behavior of the man that changes his emotional state. It is not the picture that shifts his mood or the woman's attention. These are only triggers that activate the mind of the man towards certain values, acceptance of himself, and love.

The mind of the man always makes the false impression that "they make him happy" or that he "needs" to be happy with her. It happens only when he considers the bond between the woman and her emotional state.

The man also doesn't know that to convey love; she's just an emotional stimulus to his mind. He may not have developed other triggers to communicate his own acceptance and affection, so for a trigger, he's reliant on a woman. If the man realizes she's just a catalyst and his job of expressing acceptance and affection is what shifts his emotional state, then the man doesn't need his wife to be glad.

Image of Perfection: What he believes he should be to be "good enough" to be loved.

Man's Hidden Image: Formed by all the stories in his mind about not being "good enough" A man fears becoming this, at the same time he believes he is already this failure.

The Inner Judge uses this image as the criteria to form self rejection and self criticism. This results in low self esteem, insecurity, and fear.

www.PathwayToHappiness.com
All Copyrights Reserved

The man seeks a woman's attention because that will be evidence that he fits into the success image in his mind. It is a way he can avoid the fear and painful self rejection of the failure image. The hidden failure image is only a mental construct in his mind.

Controlling actions

The man works from the mistaken assumption that a woman's affection and love make him happier. He responds with anxiety when he imagines that her focus is on someone or something other than himself.

Much of the fear isn't about losing the woman, as he may believe falsely. Most fear is about preventing the emotional pain which he produces with the Hidden Image in his head.

His beliefs in the Hidden Image become true without her knowledge. The perception of himself, too, shifts towards perceiving from this "not good enough" state. His feelings of indignity and unhappiness suit his model of belief and point of view.

The man tries to get the attention of the woman and control it so that the values of the Projected Image are involved. He's working to "disable" her "trigger" to help his confidence in the Projected Image. This is the way he uses to escape his emotionally negative feelings about the Hidden Picture. He is not conscious that love and acceptance is the concept that is the way to shift his emotional state.

Anger and punishment to control actions

One of the ways that we learn early in life is to regulate the attention and actions of other people through the anger emotion. Rage also followed the retribution, as we were disciplined as children. Even harsh words were enough to make us change a behavior. This had our attention at the very least when someone was mad at us. In this way, we learnt early in life to make use of anger as a means of regulating the attention of others, and as a punishment for regulating actions. As we got older, this habit was not automatically unlearned.

The jealous man makes use of resentment towards his partner to get her attention and control it. Rage often serves as a punishment resulting in emotional pain inflicted on the woman. By punishing the woman with rage, the woman could change her actions to escape potential emotional punishment.

The utilization of rage by the man may not be his preferred option. But his wrathful conduct is the product of a system of false beliefs. At the level of his intellect, the man may "think" differently, but his action is focused on the false beliefs and secret image that drive his emotions.

The actual outcome of controlling anger

The man gets the opposite outcome with his rage that he was programmed to become as a child. The adult usually has the ability to avoid the rage penalty than a child does. Because of their propensity to avoid the emotionally uncomfortable, the woman would withdraw from him. Her removal would then trigger his belief in the Hidden Image he tried to escape. The process of creed-emotion returns to the beginning of the individual. This is profoundly distressing.

The analysis after the incident

After an incident of envy and rage, there is an opportunity to look at the incidents and to evaluate them. This period can sometimes be more emotionally painful for the jealous man. This is when his judgment on himself can be at its worst.

The man plays rage and control behavior in his head. And it is now being checked in his mind from the Inner Judge's point of view. The Inner Judge does and rejects the study. Specifically, the Inner Judge holds up the Projected Image and then points out that "he has failed" to live up to the level. He can only assume, based on the Predicted Picture Quality, that he is a failure and not good enough.

As viewed by the Inner Judge, the rage event is "proof" that he is, in fact, the person who fits the definition of the Hidden Picture. Accepting this decision and accepting it results in the man feeling worthless, guilty, and ashamed. The Secret Image character's conviction, sentiment, and point of view is strengthened. The Inner Judge doesn't give the man a fair trial. It's a Judge on hold. The Inner Judge does not determine the position of the Belief System, False Images, or the View Point. In his view, the man is at the hands of powers that he was not equipped to see and deal with. He will begin to get control of his emotional state with knowledge of these powers and some practical practice.

Efforts to alter actions do not seem to work

The underlying issue in the study is that the man approaches the events from a judgmental point of view. Judgment leads to dismissal. It also operates to reinforce trust in the Excellence ideal. This interpretation reflects the Hidden Picture and the values of the Projected Picture that are part of the central cause. In reality, the very part of our mind that does the research confirms the core triggers.

The man is searching for a solution, and in this model of indignity, the solution looks like he should become the "Projected Picture." If he can become the positive, strong, caring, and loving person, he "knows" he is, then he will love himself, and the woman will love him, and everything will be perfect. He does not see that his imagination shapes the Projected Image.

There are other issues with this approach

1. The man's belief that he is the Expected Picture is compromised by his belief that he is not "good enough." Being great will often make up for it, but the feeling of indignity can permeate until the Secret picture is dealt with.

2. Even when the man pulls off being the ideal Projected Image, the values of the Secret Image will sound like a hoax to some of him. He is not really "good," and he is not "worthy," according to the Hidden picture beliefs. Because of these contradictory views, he can feel unauthentic. The sensation of being a cheat also arises when people are celebrating his achievements. The more success and praise he gets that suits the Imagined Image, the more

pronounced the Secret Image brings up suspicions in his mind. As long as he connects his identity with one or more contradictory images in his mind, he cannot be in Moral Honesty.

3. The man's ability to control his emotions will continually keep him on guard against an eruption of resentment and rage. This feeling of "on watch" is born out of fear that he will fall at any moment, and that emotion will consume his attention. Not only does this feeling of fear wear on a person, but it also suppresses emotion and does not allow a genuine feeling of love and happiness.

4. Creating strong positive values and a good self-image will help to minimize but, to a limited degree, the reaction side. It is a fix that can support but bases identity in a false picture and not

in honesty and dignity for others. This does nothing to resolve the feelings that emerge through the Hidden Images or indignity convictions that are at the heart of the behavior. These also get lost in the subconscious and resurface later when they become most damaging during periods of stress when we are least able to cope with them.

Emotion and false assumptions influence behavior

The behavior does not make sense when one looks at the actions of envy and rage as a way of influencing and maintaining others. Rage and envy won't make anyone want to get next to us. Often the man in the situation will look at his own behavior and see that it makes no sense. He's going to see the woman break from him as a result of his actions. And seeing the findings and knowing scientifically it will not change the essence of his behavior. Why does this happen? What for?

His behavior is not motivated by thought, reasoning, or logical comprehension. And it can't alter these modalities. This is motivated by biases, false perceptions, points of view, and emotions. When we want to improve our behavior, these fundamental concepts must be viewed differently from plain knowledge and reasoning. Why would one with knowledge and reasoning have a specific approach? To take decisions and uphold false beliefs, the Interior Judge must use reasoning and logic.

A WAY WITH RESULTS

Changing your convictions, emotional responses, and negative habits is by changing your point of view, focus, and dissolving the mind's false beliefs. You can actually push yourself out of a conviction and out of emotion as you learn to change your point of view. With a different view, you'll have the insight to see behind the actions the flawed reasoning of the convictions. Being aware of the false beliefs behind your acts will encourage you to refrain from destructive behavior. Eliminating false beliefs removes emotional triggers. Eliminating false beliefs is what will remove the terror.

If you have sufficient desire to change a jealous and angry behavior, you will ultimately have to do not just research on this, but more.

CHAPTER 8 - CODEPENDENCY (RELATIONSHIP ADDICTION)

Codependency is a state of conduct in a relationship where one person allows addiction, poor mental health, immaturity, irresponsibility, or under-realization for another.

An unhealthy reliance on other people for acceptance and a sense of identity are among the core features of codependency. Codependency definitions vary but are commonly characterized as a state of subclinical, situational, and/or episodic characters similar to that of dependent personality disorder. The word is less analytical, individually, and more descriptive of a complex relationship.

A codependent relationship in its simplest terms is when one partner needs the other partner, who needs to be needed in turn. This circular relation is the basis of what experts refer to when they define the codependency "loop."

The self-esteem and self-worth of the codependent will only come from sacrificing themselves for their mate, who is only too glad to accept their sacrifices.

Codependency Fast Facts:
Codependent relationships may be between friends, romantic partners, or family members.

Sometimes, emotional or physical violence is part of the relationship.

Friends and family members of a co-dependent individual may believe something is wrong.

As with any mental or emotional health problem, care requires time, commitment, and the assistance of a clinician.

Codependence vs. dependency

In code-dependence, one person prioritizes their needs over those of the other.

Knowing the difference between being dependent on another person — which can be a positive and beneficial trait — and being detrimental to codependency is crucial.

Below are some examples that explain the difference: Dependent: for support and affection, two people rely on each other. In relation, both find value.

Codependent: The code-dependent individual feels useless because they are needed by the enabler, and make drastic sacrifices for it. The enabler gets the satisfaction that the other person meets their every need.

The codependent is only satisfied when their partner makes serious sacrifices. They feel this other person has to need them to have some meaning.

Dependent: Both parties prioritize their partnership, yet may find pleasure in external interests, other mates, and hobbies.

Codependent: The codependent has no real identity, goals, or beliefs beyond their relationship of codependence.

Dependent: Both parties should communicate their feelings and desires and find ways for both of them to make the relationship beneficial.

Codependent: One person feels unimportant and does not express their desires and needs. They might have difficulty knowing anything about their own thoughts or needs.

Codependence can be between one or both parties. An individual who is codependent may overlook other important areas of their lives to satisfy their partner. Their intense commitment to this one person will damage their everyday obligations in other relationships. The position of an enabler is often unstable. An individual relying on a codependent does not know how to have an equal two-sided relationship, and therefore comes to rely on the sacrifices and needs of another individual.

Codependence symptoms

It can be difficult to differentiate between a person who is co-dependent and one who is only clingy or really enamored with someone else. But typically, a person who is co-dependent will:

a. find no joy or pleasure in life other than doing things for the other person.

b. Stay in the relationship when they know their partner is doing hurtful things.

c. Do whatever you want to please and fulfill your enabler no matter what the cost to you.

d. Feel intense uncertainty about their relationship because they still wish to make the other person happy.

e. Using all their time and resources to give everything they ask their partner for.

f. Feel guilty in the relationship of talking about yourself, and do not express any personal wishes or desires.

g. Ignore the other person's own values or morality for doing what he wants.

Other people may try to address their problems with the Codependent. But even though others say the person is too dependent, it would be difficult for a person in a co-dependent relationship to leave the relationship.

The codependent person may feel Intense conflict about removing himself from the enabler because his own identity depends on sacrificing himself for the other person.

What is the nature of a codependent relationship?

Codependency is an acquired trait that typically stems from past behavioral habits and emotional problems. Once thought of it as being the product of living with an alcoholic parent.

Researchers now claim that codependency can come from a number of circumstances. Some of which are:

Undermining parental relationships

Alcohol, narcotics, or other addictions are common factors that cause parents to prioritize their needs over their children's. As adults, this may trigger the children to become codependent.

Those who are codependent as adults also had issues with their infant or teenage parental relationship.

They may have been told that their own needs were less important than the needs of their parents, or not at all relevant.

In these families, the child can be taught to concentrate on the needs of the parent and never worry about himself.

Needy parents will tell their children that if they want something for themselves, the children are selfish or greedy.

As a result, the child learns to neglect his or her own needs and thinks instead about what they can still do for others.

In these circumstances, one of the parents may have:

an alcohol or drug abuse problem, a lack of maturity, and emotional growth, resulting in their own self-centered needs. These conditions trigger differences in the child's emotional growth, causing them to later pursue co-dependent relationships.

Living with a family member who is mentally or physically ill

Codependency can also arise from caring for a person who is chronically ill. Being in the caregiver role, particularly at a young age, may lead the young person to neglect their own needs and develop a habit of only helping others.

The self-worth of a person can be built around being wanted by another person and getting nothing in return.

Most people with a sick family member are not codependent. Nonetheless, it may occur in these family environments, especially if the child's parent or caregiver exhibits the above dysfunctional behaviors.

Abusive physical, mental, and sexual abuse families may cause psychological issues that last years or even a lifetime. Codependency is one of the many problems which may emerge from past violence.

An abused child or adolescent may learn to repress his or her emotions as a defense mechanism against the pain of violence. When an adult, this learned pattern leads to only thinking for the feelings of others and not understanding their own needs.

Often an abused person will later seek out abusive relationships as they are only familiar with this form of relationship. Through codependent partnerships, thls also manifests itself.

Treatment

Patient or group therapy can be more effective than couple therapy, as it allows the person to discuss their emotions and actions outside the relationship as an entity.

Many factors may help to shape a positive, healthy relationship: people in co-dependent relationships will need to take small steps in the relationship toward some separation. They may need to pursue an activity or hobby outside the relationship they enjoy.

A person who is codependent will seek to spend time with family members or friends who support him.

The enabler must realize that by encouraging them to make drastic sacrifices, they are not supporting their codependent partner.

Personal or group counseling is a great benefit to people in codependent relationships. A specialist may assist them in seeking ways to understand and communicate their emotions, which may have been hidden since childhood.

People who have been abused will have to accept past trauma and start expressing their own feelings and desires again.

Eventually, all partners must learn to identify common behavior patterns in a co-dependent relationship, such as "needing to be wanted" and requiring the other individual to center their lives around them.

Such measures are not easy to do but are worth the effort to help both parties learn how to be in a two-sided, respectful partnership.

CHAPTER 9 - OVERCOMING JEALOUSY

The steps to overcome jealous responses on a permanent basis are: to recover personal power so you can control your feelings and stop reactive behavior.

Change your point of view, so that in your mind you can step back from the story. It will allow you a time gap to stop a jealous or angry reaction and do something else.

Identify the core beliefs which activate the emotional response.

Be mindful that your mental convictions aren't valid. That is different from intellectually "knowing" that the stories are not true.

Build power over your focus so you can choose consciously which story is playing in your mind and which emotions you experience.

11 Ways to resolve insecurities in a relationship

There are moments when you still don't know that you're not good enough even when you think you've found the love of your life. Sometimes you even feel those bouts of insecurity that not only trigger an argument between you and your significant other but also affect your self-esteem.

Persons who are not really aware of their worth as an individual, as a lover, and as a life partner often experience insecurities in a relationship. There are, however, things and practices that can support someone who suffers from this negative emotional wave by following and trusting in the various ways of resolving uncertainties, particularly in romantic relationships.

So, what are the steps you should be taking to make your relationship feel more secure? They are as follows.

1. **Stop comparing yourself to someone else.**

Particularly with your other important former lovers. It's one of the causes of fighting between couples, and although it can be normal and sometimes reasonable, there are people who always still find a way to make it a problem, even if the triggers are nowhere to be seen.

Insecurity and envy are a lethal combination and can either build or destroy the relationship as couples resolve the issues that come with this mixture.

2. **Start appreciating your uniqueness.**

You're different, and you're not like anybody else. Remember that, man. Yet some people don't know the positive stuff about them, and sometimes they hate themselves because they don't feel different. It is another form of vulnerability and the most prevalent.

The best way to overcome this self-hatred is to realize that there are people who truly appreciate your very existence. Second, and more importantly, you have someone on your side who loves you just like you do.

3. **Don't fear to ask the right questions.**

One of the origins of insecurity has something to do with the reality, the answers we're too scared to hear from questions we won't dare ask – due to lack of trust and low self-esteem.

Often the desire to know the truth about issues that describe us as a person and lover can lead to confusion, anxiety, and sometimes overthink.

4. **Build your trust here.**

Occasionally, the root cause of insecurities is not what someone doesn't possess but their inability to see what's already in their front: their talents and their own goodness, which were the reasons why a particular someone fell in love with them first. So, how can the blindness be cured? In that, be assured.

Believe in yourself, and let faith scare off those insecurities. How is it? There are different ways of being confident and proud of who you are and what you are. You just need to have the courage to open your eyes.

5. **Place your confidence in others more.**

Another source of fear is our inability to trust others because of previous experiences that have led us to believe you can't depend on someone other than you. Let them go and open themselves in your life to new people, create a community, and be with the crowd.

Stop building those walls, hoping they'd shield you from the outside world's cruelties. Instead, leave more doors and windows open, so others 'lights will make your life brighter.

6. **Find out what makes you particularly angry.**

We've listed a number of root causes of insecurity, particularly in relation to people. Most of the more basic reasons a person may feel unsafe; however, really depend on a variety of factors.

Find out what makes you particularly angry. Find the causes, the stuff, and the things that can make you experience the bad. In other words, be more conscious of yourself, particularly the wrong pieces.

7. **Accept things you can't change.**

Don't grieve over the things you can never get back to, the realities that you can't change in your relationship. One of the causes of insecurity is our failure to realize that the challenges we see and experience with your significant others are part of our lives. You can still make it better, however.

Start by seeing yourself and reacting to the challenges, events, and interactions that come your way. Do you respond in anger? Lived in anxiety? And are you embracing them with a sort of wisdom that will help you cope and survive?

8. **Change your attitude towards life and towards men.**

If you think nothing is improving in relation to the previous section, and you still feel disappointment and frustration in your relationship, maybe all you need is a change of perspective? As the popular saying goes, if you like your reality, change it; otherwise, change your attitude.

We realize that it is easier said than done, but we must all start somewhere, aren't we? Get it done right now.

9. **Find your strengths and grow them.**

Instead of dwelling on the bad and the negative, find something inside yourself that you can build and draw strength from. For example, you could try to find out what makes you glad as an individual, as a partner to your significant other, or as a friend in your circle.

Realize the good things about yourselfvia those people who really care about you. They're your permanent source of strength. Keep them close to you.

10. **Value the people around you right now.**

Talking about getting your loved ones and friends around to help you rediscover the positive things about yourself, it's important you consider doing the same for them. Respect them by demonstrating how important you are, and why they are important to you.

In return, people who give love and who are loved never fall victim to the bloody gloom of insecurity. They know what they are worth, and they trust the people they love will be there to remind them how special they are, even if they don't feel their best.

11. **Love yourself, please.**

Last but not least, love yourself. Even if you're in a romantic relationship where you're expected to give love, never forget to love yourself.

Remember never to let good things happen to you just because you have not been able to appreciate your own value. The feeling of insecurity and the negativity that comes with it is a common relationship between killers. Do something like that before it's too late.

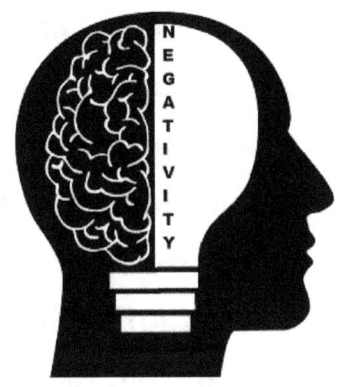

Negative thoughts could lie with us, with others, with our situation and the world, with the past, with the future. Many times, if they have low self-esteem with stress and fear depression and other people's treatment of us, people are used to negative thoughts, but we can also intensify these emotional states if we don't recognize our habits and don't question them.

For example, if you often think, "I'm useless," you're likely to sink into a depressed mood and/or withdraw from people, so they don't see how useless you are.

When you are lonely, isolated, and depressed, you are more likely to think negatively: your mood affects your thoughts, and your isolation means that you are not around other people who could directly or indirectly contradict your opinion of yourself. And in a vicious circle, you may be trapped. Banning negative thinking will lead to a happier mindset, a greater trust in oneself, more positive ways of living, and stronger relationships through practice.

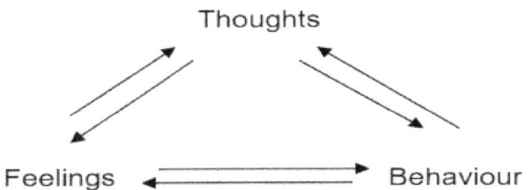

Thoughts

Feelings ⟷ Behaviour

There are two steps to banish negative thoughts: **IDENTIFY them and CHALLENGING them in your mind.**

IDENTIFYING NEGATIVE THOUGHTS

There are a number of common patterns of negative thinking. Take one of your regular negative thoughts and see if it fits in one or more of the following patterns.

1. All or Nothing Thinking doesn't allow any middle ground – if something doesn't go perfectly, it's "complete failure." You're "ugly" if you don't look like a model. If your presentation wasn't "brilliant," it was "rubby." You

may even use words inside your head when you think, like, "always, never, nobody, all the time," etc.

2. Over-generalizing exaggerates the specific facts – if two girlfriends in a row end up with you, you think to yourself, "women always dump me in the end." It can lead to labeling as a result – if you have backed out of a couple of romantic situations and then label yourself as "female / male hopeless" or "total coward." Labels don't help us feel good about ourselves or about the possibility of change!

3. Mental Filtering is presented with a mass of information, but it is presented solely on the negative parts of it and ignores the rest. So maybe you're writing your CV, and you're going to end up depressed because you're worried about the lack of work

experience or your A-level grades. At the same time, overlooking absolutely the fact that you have done a lot of volunteering work.

4. Discounting Positive is similar to that of mental filtering. It's when: a) you notice or acknowledge your positive qualities or achievements, but you won't count them as important or celebrate them. "Well, yes, I got a 2:1 mark for that assignment, but it was just a fluke." "Yes, three people told me I look pretty today, but they're just saying that to cheer me up."b) you're not even aware of your positive qualities or achievements.

5. Crystal Ball, or "Fortune Telling," is talking to you as if you have the privilege of knowing what the future holds if you don't! "I'm never going to find anyone"; "I feel compelled to have

a house party," she says. "I project negative thoughts and memories from the past and the present as if they will eventually linger with you or replicate themselves.

6. In your mind it is believed you know what others are or would think if you did not say something or they were not there; you might also make an picture of a future occurrence in your head, and then assume that the picture reflects what is going happen "for certain." "They think I'm dull," "they assume I should have come back with her," or "he's going to think I'm sorry to be able to ask him to help me."

7. When you see your negative emotions as evidence of yourself and your condition, emotional reasoning is. It also could contribute to "I have to be depressed constantly; I have to be a sad guy." "I'm

guilty, so I have to do the wrong thing" or, "I think I'm so bad that I have to be a bad person. It can also lead to labels like" I'm always depressed; I have to be a depressed person.

8. Personalization (sometimes referred to as misallocation) is when you mentally take responsibility for something that wasn't or isn't your responsibility. "It's my fault that he was so bad to me at that seminar, I was supposed to keep quiet;" "It's my fault that Mum was so ill, I was supposed to take a year out and stay at home."

9. Well, what iffing.

It will lift your worry when you say to yourself, "What if ...?" "What if I fail to follow the plan," etc. 'What if he breaks up with me?

IDENTIFYING THE TYPE OF THOUGHTS HELP YOU TO DISTANCE YOURSELF

SLIGHTLY AND GAIN THE PERSPECTIVE REQUIRED TO CHALLENGE THEM

CHALLENGING NEGATIVE THOUGHTS

You challenge your thinking by questioning how valid/true/rational it is, and there are different ways of questioning that can be used alone or in combination.

1. Will I have ample knowledge to say this? Will my knowledge of reality reveal any noticeable gaps? Could I think of something else if I knew more? If so, stop negative thinking and get the truth!

2. What proof does this concept provide? AND WHAT About IS EVIDENCE? In the light of all the facts, have I reached a fair and equal point of view? If not, what is a fairer, more accurate approach?

3. (What are the practical chances of this happening for fears of something negative going on in the future? Am I overestimating my chances because of my fear? What other likely outcomes are there? Have I underestimated my own ability to cope with a possible difficulty?

4. Am I in the habit of thinking about this? How did I learn about this habit? Am I just going to repeat the put-downs that someone/others in my past gave me? In their assessment of me, were they objective and fair?

5. Would my best friend be in agreement with my thinking? If I had been a relative, would I have been less harsh on this situation than me? Should I have a standard for other individuals and another standard for myself — do

I presume I am perfect? If I am, will I make myself happy or unhappy?

6. Answering any "What if?" questions you're asking. If you can answer "What if" then you will generate a number of options that may help you reduce your anxiety.

BANISHING NEGATIVE THOUGHTS

Once you analyze and question your thoughts as mentioned, you can replace them with ideas that are more constructive, or at least more logical and objective. You may remove their self- or self- tone. As well as the emotional relief, your attitude and self- over time can be increased by a more optimistic view about yourself and / or your situation. It is a method that must be learned and practiced with many people to counter the negative thoughts and replace them with positive ones. Don't give it up! With time, you'll get better and better to catch your self-critical, fearful, pessimistic thoughts, and to evaluate, challenge, and change them more quickly.

JOHN BOWLBY ATTACHMENT

The attachment is a deep and enduring emotional bond that connects one person to another through time and space. Attachment needn't be mutual. One person can have an unshared connection to an entity.

Attachment is characterized by particular behaviors in children, such as seeking closeness when distressed or threatened to an attachment (Bowlby, 1969); Attachment activity in adults to the infant includes responsively and respectfully listening to the child's needs. Such behavior is common across cultures. The Attachment Theory offers an overview of how the bond between parent and child evolves and affects future developments.

Attachment theory of psychology originates from John Bowlby's seminal work (1958). John Bowlby worked as a psychiatrist at the London Child Guidance Clinic in the 1930s, where he examined several children who had become mentally disturbed. This experience led Bowlby to recognize the social, emotional, and cognitive developmental significance of the children's relationship with their mother. Specifically, he shaped his belief in the relationship between early infant separation from the mother and later maladjustment and led Bowlby to form his theory of attachment. John Bowlby, working with James Robertson (1952), found that when separated from their mothers, the children suffered extreme distress. And when other carers were feeding these babies, the child's anxiety did not diminish. Such results defied the prevailing theory of behavioral attachment (Dollard and Miller, 1950), which had been shown to underestimate the bond between the child and his mother. Attachment behavior theory suggested the infant had become attached to the mother as she had fed the baby. Bowlby defined attachment as a "lasting psychological relationship between human beings." Bowlby (1958) suggested that attachment could be understood in an evolutionary context in that the caregiver provides safety and security for the infant. Attachment is adaptive as it increases the chance of survival of the infant. This is illustrated in the works of Lorenz (1935) and Harlow (1958). According to Bowlby infants, there is a universal need to seek close proximity to their caregivers when they are under stress or at risk (Glaser & Prior, 2006). Many researchers think attachment develops through a variety of stages.

Stages of Attachment

Rudolph Schaffer and Peggy Emerson (1964) observed 60 children in the first 18 months of life at monthly intervals (this is regarded as a longitudinal study). The children were all examined at home, and a normal pattern of development of attachment was established. The babies were seen for about a year on a monthly basis, their interactions with their carers were examined, and the carers interviewed. The mother kept a diary to examine the evidence for the development of the attachment.

Three measures have been recorded:

Stranger's anxiety-response to the arrival of a stranger.

Separation Anxiety-the level of distress when separated from the carer, the degree of comfort needed on return.

Social Reference- the degree that the child looks at the caregiver to check how they are supposed to respond to something new (secure base).

They found out that the attachments of the child develop in the following sequence:

asocial (0-6 weeks)

Very young infants are asocial in that many kinds of stimuli, both social and not, produce a favorable reaction, such as a smile.

Indiscriminate Attachments (6 weeks to 7 months)

Children enjoy a human company without discrimination, and most babies respond equally to any caregiver. They get upset when an individual stop interacting with them. From 3 months of age, infants smile more at familiar faces and can be easily comforted by a regular caregiver.

Specific attachment (7-9 months)

Special preference for a single attachment number. The child looks for stability, comfort, and safety for particular people. It shows the fear of strangers and unhappiness when they are separated from a particular person.). Some babies show anxieties of stranger fear and separation more frequently and intensely than others, but nonetheless, they are seen as evidence that the child has formed an attachment. Usually, this has developed by one year of age.

Multiple Attachment (10 months and upwards)

The child is ever more confident and develops many attachments. Most babies have multiple attachments by the 18th month. The study results showed that associations were more likely to develop with those who correctly responded to the children's signals, not the person they spent most time with. Schaffer and Emerson called for the critical responsiveness. Intensely attached infants had mothers who quickly reacted to their demands and interacted with their kids. The infants who were weakly attached had mothers who had not been able to interact. Many of the babies had more than ten months old attachments, including attachments to mothers, fathers, grandparents, siblings, and neighbors. The mother was the main figure of attachment for about half of the children aged 18 months and the father for most of the others. The most important thing in the formation of attachments isn't about who feeds and changes the child, but about who plays and communicates with him or her. Hence, responsiveness seemed to be the key to attachment.

Attachment Theory

Psychologists have suggested two key hypotheses that are considered significant in attachment formation.

Learning / behavioral theory of attachment (e.g., Dollard & Miller, 1950) implies attachment is a collection of learned habits. The supply of food is the basis from which attachments are formed. At first, an infant may develop an attachment to the person who feeds it. We learn to equate the feeder (usually the mother) with the comfort of being fed and to come into contact with the nurturing mother through the classical conditioning cycle. They often notice that some behaviors (e.g., crying, smiling) attract favorable responses from others (e.g., attention, comfort) and learn to replicate certain behaviors through the operating conditioning cycle to get the things they want.

Evolutionary attachment theory (e.g., Bowlby, Harlow, Lorenz) suggests that children come into the world biologically pre-programmed to form attachments with others because that will help them survive. The infant produces innate 'social liberator' behaviors such as crying and smiling, which stimulate the innate response of adults to care giving. The defining attachment factor isn't food, but treatment and responsiveness. Bowlby proposed that initially, the child should develop only one primary attachment (monotropy) and that the attachment figure should serve as a stable foundation for exploring the world. The attachment relationship serves as a blueprint for all possible social interactions, and it can have significant implications. This theory also suggests a crucial time (around 0-5 years) for the development of an attachment. During this time, the infant will experience irreversible psychological consequences as intelligence declines and aggression, if an attachment has not formed.

Harlow's Monkeys (1958)

Harlow decided to research newborn rhesus monkeys 'processes of interconnectedness. They were highly dependent on their mothers for nutrition, protection, comfort, and socialization. But what, exactly, was the basis of the bond? Behavioral attachment theory would suggest that an infant would form an attachment to a carer providing food. On the other hand, Harlow's explanation was that attachment grows as a result of the mother providing "tactile comfort," suggesting that babies have an inbuilt (biological) need to touch and hold on to something for emotional comfort. Harry Harlow did various attachment studies in rhesus monkeys in the 1950s and 1960s. His experiments took a number of forms:

Baby monkeys grown in isolation

He took baby monkeys and separated them from birth. These monkeys didn't have any contact with each other or anyone else. Most of them lived this way for three months, others for six months, some for nine months, and some for their first year of life. He then placed them back to see what effect their inability to establish attachment has on their actions with other monkeys.

Results: Apes engaged in bizarre behavior, such as clutching their own bodies and rocking compulsively. They were then put back in the company of the other monkeys. The babies were afraid of the other monkeys to begin with, and then they were very violent towards them. We still did not interact with other monkeys or socialize with them. They were bullied by the other monkeys. They indulged in self-mutilation, tearing their hair out, scratching, and biting their own arms and legs.

Harlow concluded that neglect is profoundly detrimental to monkeys (i.e., never establishing an attachment bond). The length of the insulation represented the severity of the abnormal behavior. The least affected were those held in solitary confinement for three months, but those in solitary confinement for one year have never regained the effects of deprivation.2. Infant monkeys raised with surrogate mothers eight monkeys were separated immediately after birth from their mothers and put in cages with access to two surrogate mothers, one made of wire and one with soft terry toweling cloth. Four of the monkeys were able to receive milk from mother wire and four from mother cloth. The animals were observed over 165 days. All groups of monkeys spent more time in their mother's cloth (even though she had no milk). The baby would go to his wire mother only if she was hungry. Once fed, the mother would go back to the cloth for most of the day. If a frightening object was placed in a cage, the infant took refuge with the mother of cloth (its safe base). This surrogate was more effective in reducing the fear of youngsters. When the mother of the cloth was present, the infant would explore more. It supports the evolutionary theory of attachment as it is necessary for the caregiver to be receptive to and healthy (as described in food supplies). The behavioral variations found by Harlow between the monkeys with surrogates and those with normal mothers have been much more passive.

b) They didn't have the slightest idea of how to manage different monkeys.

c) They were easily bullied and would not stand up for themselves.

d) They had difficulty getting married.

(e) The females were not sufficient mothers.

These behaviors have been observed only in monkeys who have been left with surrogate mothers for more than 90 days. For those less than 90 days left, the effects could be reversed if they were put in a normal environment where they could form attachments. Harlow came to a conclusion that, in order for a monkey to develop normally, he / she must have some interaction with an object to which they may cling during the first months of his / her life (critical period). Clinging is a natural response-in times of stress, the monkey runs to the object to which it normally clings as if clinging reduces stress. He also concluded that early maternal neglect would cause emotional damage but that if the attachment was made prior to the end of the critical period, its effect could be reversed in monkeys. Nevertheless, if maternal neglect continued after the crucial time ended, no amount of access to mothers or peers could change the already occurring emotional damage. Harlow, therefore, found that it was social deprivation rather than maternal deprivation that the baby monkeys suffered. When he raised some other monkeys on his own, but with twenty minutes a day in a playroom with three other monkeys, he noticed that they grew up to be quite normal, both emotionally and socially.

Ethics of Harlow's Study

Harlow's work has been criticized. While seeking to explain the effects of deprivation on human children, his findings were seen as unnecessarily cruel (unethical) and of little interest. Through this research, it became evident that the monkeys had experienced emotional damage from being born through isolation. This became obvious when the monkeys were put in a corner huddled in a state of constant fear and depression, with a typical monkey (reared by a mother).

Additionally, Harlow, in female monkeys, developed a state of anxiety that had consequences when they became parents. Such monkeys were so neurotic that they smashed the face of their child and rubbed it back and forth to the surface. Harlow's experiment is often justified as a valuable insight into how attachment and social behavior evolves. There was a prevalent assumption at the time of the research that attachment was more related to physical (i.e., food) than to emotional treatment. The benefits of the study may be claimed to outweigh the costs (animal suffering). For example, the theoretical work of John Bowlby, the most influential psychologist in attachment theory, has been influenced by the study. Convincing people about the importance of emotional treatment in schools, children's homes, and day treatment may also be seen as important.

Lorenz's Imprinting Theory

Lorenz (1935) took and held a large clutch of goose eggs until they were about to hatch. Half of the eggs were then put under a goose mother, while Lorenz kept the other half for a few hours by himself. When the geese hatched, Lorenz imitated the quacking sound of the mother duck, which the young birds considered their mother, and followed him accordingly. The other group followed the mother of the goose. Lorenz found that the geese followed the first moving object they saw during a critical 12- hour period after the hatching. This process is known as imprinting and indicates that the attachment is innate and genetically programmed. Imprinting has implications for both the short- survival and, in the longer term, the formation of internal templates for future relationships. Imprinting occurs without any feeding. If no attachment has formed within 32 hours, any attachment would unlikely ever develop. Lorenz placed all the goslings under the box to ensure the imprinting and allowed them to mix. The two classes were separated when the box was removed to transfer half to the goose of their mothers and a half to Lorenz. Impressions do not appear to be involved immediately after hatching, but there is a critical time in which impressions can occur. Hess (1958) found that while the imprinting process could take place as early as one hour after hatching, the strongest reactions occurred between 12 and

17 hours after hatching and that the reaction was unlikely to occur at all after 32 hours. Lorenz and Hess claim that it cannot be changed after an imprint has taken place, nor can the gosling imprint something else on it. Most people grow up worrying about abandonment. Some of them have been plagued by these fears quite consistently throughout their lives. They are worried that peers, partners, schools, companies, or entire social circles will be rejected. For many others, these fears are not fully realized until they enter into a romantic relationship. Things are going smoothly, and all of a sudden, they feel inundated with insecurity and fear that their partner will distance themselves, ignore them, or leave them.

Everyone is experiencing this fear at various levels. Most of us can relate to having heightened anxiety over the thoughts of rejection. We may be set off by anything from a long first date to a long- partner who seems distracted and not available.

In severe cases, people may struggle with "auto phobia," a huge fear of being alone or isolated, which makes them feel that they are ignored or uncared for even when they are with another person. They may also experience fear of abandonment phobia, which is characterized by extreme dependence on other people, it is commonly present among individuals that are diagnosed with borderline personality disorders.

The extent to which a person is faced with this fear can shape how they live their lives and experience their relationships. There are, however, effective ways for people to develop more security within themselves and overcome their fear of abandonment. They can begin by understanding where this fear originates from.

Where does fear of abandonment come from?

As adolescents, people suffer real losses, rejections, or traumas that make them feel insecure and distrustful of the world. Such setbacks and traumas may be devastating, such as the death of a loved one, neglect, or emotional and physical violence.

Nevertheless, they may also occur at a far more subtle level in the day-to-day interactions between parents and children. For children to feel comfortable, they need to feel protected, seen and soothed when they're upset. It has been said, however, that even the best of parents are only completely attuned to their children about 30% of the time. Exploring their early stages of an attachment may provide individuals with insight into their perceptions of loss and rejection. Understanding how their parents relate to them, and if they have encountered a stable relationship versus an unstable one, will give people insight as to how they see relationships in the present.

Safe attachments develop when caregivers are regularly available and attuned to the needs of the infant. However, ruptures in such early relationships may lead children to unsafe attachments. From childhood, people learn to behave in ways that better meet the needs of their parents or caregivers. A parent who may at one time be present and meet the needs of the child, but at another time be totally unavailable and turn away or, on the other hand, disruptive and "emotionally hungry" may lead the child to develop an ambivalent / anxiety pattern of attachment. Kids who undergo this kind of dependence appear to feel insecure. We can cling to the parent in an attempt to meet their needs. However, they can also fail to feel at ease with the parent. They are sometimes nervous and unsure about the parent, who is unpredictable in their conduct, often accessible and caring, and sometimes disrespectful or intrusive in ways that frustrate the child.

Why early attachment patterns and feelings of loss impact us in adulthood

The early attachment experience of an individual serves as an internal working model for how he or she wants relationships to function. As a result, people can have their childhood insecurities and assumptions about how others should act in their adult relationships. Children who experience an ambivalent pattern of attachment that develop to have a preoccupied pattern of attachment as adults in which they tend to feel insecure in their relationships. "They sometimes feel helpless and assume the role of 'pursuer' in a relationship," wrote Joyce Catlett, co-author of Compassionate Child Rearing. "They depend heavily on their partner to affirm their self-esteem. Since they grew up insecure due to the inconsistent availability of their caregivers, they are 'rejection-sensitive.' They expect rejection or abandonment and search for indications that their partner is losing interest." Adults who experience fear of abandonment that struggle with a preoccupied attachment style. They also fear rejection and discover signs of disinterest from their partner. We may feel triggered by even subtle or perceived signs of rejection on the part of their partner based on the actual rejections we encountered in their childhood. As a consequence, they can behave possessively, in charge, jealously, or clinging to their partner. They will also seek reassurance or show mistrust. "However, their excessive dependence, demands, and possessiveness seem to backfire and precipitate the very abandonment they fear," Catlett wrote. He explains how certain people who fear rejection act in ways that are punitive, resentful, and angry when their partner doesn't give them the attention and reassurance, they think they need to feel safe. "They also feel that when they convey their fear and frustration dramatically, it is impossible that the other individual will react to them," Catlett wrote. However, some people with preoccupied relationships are more "reluctant to communicate their angry feelings towards a partner out of fear of possible failure or rejection." This could lead them to suppress their feelings, which may cause them to build up and ultimately spill out in outbursts of intense emotion. If they repress or express their intense feelings, these individuals are activated in the present on the basis of past events. Resolving these feelings is also the secret to becoming better about oneself and having healthy relationships.

The early attachment style of a person may also influence the choice of his or her partner. People also select partners that match their past trends. For example, if they feel neglected as adolescents, they can select a partner who is self-centered or distant. People are rarely aware of this phase, but they may feel an extra attraction to someone who reminds them of their history. Or you will find ways to recreate your childhood's emotional climate. People who fear being also discarded not only choose partners that are less eligible, but may also misrepresent their partners, thinking that they are more rejected than they are. Eventually, they often encourage the other person to step back and build more space in ways that affect their partner—picking on the trends that Drs. Robert and Lisa Firestone's call for "range, exaggeration, and provocation" will help people who fear loss make better choices that can help them build more protection.

How can the fear of abandonment be overcome and change our attachment patterns?

Luckily, the style of attachment of an individual is not set. We may build won stable attachment as adults in a variety of ways. As Dr. Lisa Firestone, who recently co- the online course Making Your Life Sense: Understanding Your Past to Free Your Present and Empower Your Future with Dr. Daniel

Siegel, said, "What is violated in a partnership will always be repaired in the partnership." This does not mean that the new partner will fill the voids or heal all of the wounds of his chili. When a person is able to form a relationship with someone who has a long history of being firmly attached to him or her, he or she may discover that he or she does not have to cling desperately to a person to meet his or her needs. Therapy is another way for individuals to build more protection within themselves. Having a stable relationship with a therapist may help the individual develop a safe attachment.

Attachment research has also shown that it is not just what happens to people in childhood that affects their adult relationship; So deeply, they feel about what happened to them and know the full pain. As people, we are not powerless victims of our backgrounds, but we have to face our past so as to build a better future. One of the most powerful ways for a person to build a strong relationship is to make sense of his or her story. Dr. Daniel Siegel speaks about the value of constructing a cohesive narrative to make people feel more comfortable and empowered within themselves. As people make sense of and express their story, they get to know their habits and their causes, and they're not as automatically reactive in a relationship – either with a romantic partner or with their children. If people have a sense of their history, they may be less likely to have such extreme, knee-jerk fear of abandonment. Yet even though they experience panic, they're much better able to calm down. We can understand where their anxiety comes from and where it belongs, so they can take action that is more logical so relevant to the nature of their current lives. We should improve and reinforce their relationships rather than respond with fear and insecurity and build the distance they fear.

Calming techniques if you are fearful of abandonment

Each one of us is afraid of being left alone. Some of us have certain underlying feelings that we are unlovable or that we will not be embraced for who we are. We all have a "strong inner voice," a negative internal dialog that constantly criticizes us or gives us bad advice. This 'voice' also perpetuates our fear of abandonment: "He's going to leave you," he says. "She's definitely cheating," she says. Since we all have "voices" and alarms that are activated when we feel triggered, it's good to have tools and techniques to calm down when we find our fears amp. One helpful guide is this toolkit to help people deal with anxiety, which outlines activities and techniques that are safe for everyone to use when they feel excited.

Another common principle to be followed is one of self-compassion. Researcher Dr. Kristin Neff has carried out research that shows many benefits of self-compassion. Enhancing self-compassion is also beneficial for building self-esteem, as self-compassion is not so much about judgment and assessment. Rather, it includes three main elements:

Self-kindness: this relates to the belief that people should be kind to themselves, as opposed to judgmental. It sounds easy, theoretically, but it's a lot more complicated in reality. The more people can have a dry, welcoming attitude towards themselves and their challenges, the better they will feel in the face of challenging circumstances. We should always be a better friend of our own, even though we feel hurt or betrayed by anyone else.

Mindfulness: Mindfulness is good, as it helps people not over-identify their thoughts and emotions in ways that encourage them to get carried away. When people feel afraid of anything like being discarded, they seem to have a lot of negative thoughts about themselves, perpetuating this fear. Imagine if you could understand these thoughts and emotions without letting them overwhelm you. Could you take a gentler approach towards yourself and let these thoughts move through like clouds in the sky instead of floating away with them – without losing your sense of self and, sometimes, reality?

Basic Humanity: The more we can accept that we are divine, and, like all human beings, the more self-compassion and resilience we can cultivate in our lives. If individuals constantly realize that they are not alone and that they are worthy, they will help themselves from believing those cruel and incorrect messages, telling them that they will be rejected or unwanted.

Moving away from the fear of abandonment

Fear of abandonment can be very painful and real, but if people can practice self-compassion, they are very likely to get through those times when they are activated. The more people in their history can trace these emotions to their origins, the more they can distinguish these memories from the present. It takes bravery for someone to be able to see what affects them and to confront the primary feelings of rejection that they might have had as children because they have no influence over their circumstances. But when people are able to confront these emotions, they will eventually set themselves free from many of the chains of their experience. They may become distinct adults who are capable of developing new stories and new relationships in which they feel protected, heard, soothed, and therefore comfortable.

To experience well-being, it is important to feel safe and comfortable in all areas of our lives. However, the biggest need for this is in our relationship. If there is security, then we're going to feel trust and protection. When, though, these emotions are threatened by the ghosts of the past, then fear will enter our lives. One of the strongest is the fear of abandonment.

The confusion that triggers the fear of being abandoned may weaken the relationship. It is particularly true when the cause of all this is a fractured and distorted childhood. Whoever harbors this irrational fear can unintentionally damage their relationship and cause their partner to confirm what they already suspected. On the other side, the relationship can become so damaging that all participants become caught in a vortex of pain and misery.

It's very natural to be scared from time to time that the relationship doesn't work. Nevertheless, living in a continuous situation of mistrust and hypersensitivity to rejection creates discomfort and instability. Let us look closely at the consequences of the fear of giving up.

The strength of the attachment bond

During the first year of life, we develop an emotional bond with our primary caregiver, known as attachment. Via this relationship and the kind of bond, we are creating, each one of us will acquire a set of emotional capacities. We will extend this to our future interpersonal relationships.

If this relation never occurs, it will trigger a lot of issues in the future. If that is the case, then our physical and emotional needs could have caused us to grow up feeling vulnerable, insecure, and distrustful. It is one of the implications discussed in Bowlby's attachment theory (see below). He describes the deep feeling of loss that many people feel, even when they are surrounded by those they love. Let's look at an instance of how to understand it better.

Starving baby

A baby is starving due to the fact that it hasn't been eaten for a few hours. His whole body tells him he's hungry. Yet the only devices he has at his fingertips are weeping and anger. His mother, as the main caregiver in this situation, catches the signs he sends and interprets that he's hungry. Why? Why? Because she's learned to identify and alleviate the physical and emotional needs of her child. This will restore the physiological and emotional equilibrium of the infant.

When the child goes through these kinds of encounters on a continuous basis, he or she will still look for physical proximity to his or her mother. He believes that she will be able to calm him down and regain his equilibrium. Later in their life, the child would be able to tolerate disturbing encounters just by seeing his mother approach him or saying, "I'll be back soon."

Despite that, when something similar happens to you when you're an adult, you're cool. You remember you'll see your family, girlfriend, or friend in a couple of hours. Your brain has discovered that it can feel relaxed and that it can be a lasting feeling.

If the infant's brain has never felt a sense of calm or expectation, after a bad experience, you will feel peace; the adult's brain will never feel peace. You're not going to feel comfortable in an intimate relationship because you haven't learned where to find peace. In addition, lack of touch and treatment results in higher production of adrenaline in the brain. This makes us act more aggressive and impulsive. This makes it impossible for us to control our feelings, too.

CHAPTER 12 - EMOTIONAL INJURIES OF ABANDONMENT IN COUPLES

As we can see, there are injuries, like a feeling of losing something, which, while we don't see them, stays in the deepest parts of us. They're capable of shaping so many aspects of our lives. Some of the experiences we encounter in childhood leave their mark on us. When they're untreated, they're capable of destroying us apart without even knowing it.

In his theory of attachment, Bowlby developed that emotional relations created in childhood continue in the form of models in the representational world of the adult. Hazan and Shave also prove this in their inquiries. They have shown that adult conduct in relationships is influenced by the mental expectations that developed in the relationship present between the child and their parents.

We can, hence, see that the fear of relationship loss is ingrained in childhood. They are the ghosts of the past which are coming back, taking with them all our fear. They're trying to tell you that you're not deserving of getting affection or good treatment from anyone. Typically, they occur because the brain receives a warning signal.

Emotional attachment

A phrase, a location, a form of action, or memory is sufficient to trigger an "emergency situation" in a person who has never been able to feel completely safe or comfortable. And there, a whole cascade of feelings and actions starts to reveal itself. Instability, apathy, depression, to mention only three.

In addition, a person who experiences fear of abandonment typically develops an emotional dependency on his or her partner. We end up in need of their daily approval. If their relationship is abusive, they would be absolutely unable to put an end to it or separate themselves. It's like they weren't without the other guy. They're capable of doing almost everything to keep the friendship going—anything, that is, except to reopen old wounds.

For certain situations, this fear of loss induces a kind of reliance on this lack of esteem and self-deprecation. When they don't feel needed or protected, they need to confirm that this identity is still there. That's why, if they really want safety and security, they end up denying it or not believing it. All this is caused by deeply rooted signs of untreated post-traumatic stress.

Fear of abandonment

Fear of abandonment is a deep emotional wound, rooted in childhood. Healing this wound requires acknowledging and forgiving the past in order to let it go. It is a dynamic mission. Especially if the person isn't conscious of the way their previous experience has conditioned them, this is also made worse by their defenses. After all, what was meant to be for their safety turns out not to be so impervious.

In reality, it is best to go to a specialist in the most complicated cases. They're going to be able to support you, particularly in the first important steps. Another thing that needs to be focused on is self-esteem. It's normally cracked, even broken. It is important to learn to value yourself to break the cycle of emotional dependency. In turn, it would be far easier to control the feelings and perceptions that are rooted in your past experiences with positive self-esteem.

Changing our emotions

Emotions such as rage, frustration, fear, or depression are very common in people who fear being abandoned. You need to know how to reduce their strength and what they really say. If you do that, you're going to be able to turn them into something constructive.

Negative beliefs and aspirations are often factors that need to be taken into account. Much of the time, our worries are on what affect and heighten our fears. They're making them even bigger than they should be. If we fear that our partner will abandon us, we will be more mindful of their actions and their words. We may also misinterpret them in order to reinforce the prejudices inside us.

As we can see, curing the fear of loss requires a cycle of restoration. This is a time-consuming operation. We need to learn to give importance to and reveal our fears.

There's something we can't think about. On several times, what we think is going on outside is nothing more than a projection of what's going on inside of us. If you can connect with any of these signs, we urge you to seek treatment and recovery before it's too late.

Communication is the key to a solid, stable relationship. In so many ways, contact allows couples to share messages about love and other emotions. Good communication includes the development of listening skills and the presentation of thoughts and feelings. It's much more than talking since communication consists of verbal signals (what you say), contextual problems (how you tell it), emotional tone (why you tell it), and non-verbal cues (what you don't say).

LISTENING

Hearing is one of the most important communication capabilities because it is your friend's best way to learn. A good listener is more than just listening to words; he interprets feelings, actions, and responds appropriately. Yet how is it that one is a strong listener?

A good listener pays attention to the words of his / her partner AND emotions, the behavior of which sends a strong message: "You are important to me." This indicates concern and increases the probability that your partner will continue to express his / her emotions. If your friend is listening, allow them to talk about what they think is important. Continue listening without prejudice or blame if you disagree with their arguments. Note that effective listening does not require defensiveness; thus, do not use it as an excuse to criticize your friend. Good communication can be the secret to unraveling the present and avoiding potential issues that may occur in a couple's relationship.

Listening allows you to pay attention to your partner's tone of voice, facial expression, eye contact, and physical movements. It is important to concentrate on non-verbal representations of feelings as well as spoken words. It's quick to be reckless and believe you know what the other person says. Others claim to listen as they're doing something else, while others clearly demonstrate that they've been zoned-out mentally. You can't concentrate on what to do next or make comparisons with what your partner said in the past to break these patterns. Give them your full attention and take some time to think before you answer. It may be difficult to improve bad listening habits, but this is possible. Improving communication is worth the effort because listening to your partner is probably the best way to show love and concern.

Habits We Have That Avoids Good Listening

As Listeners

Habits and actions in the past have become more difficult to listen to. We too often concentrate, as listeners, on the response we should give — rather than concentrating on the message we receive. Our custom of worrying or jumping into conclusions takes the desired message away.

Judgmental behavior takes this bad practice a step further, putting another roadblock to successful communication. A fast answer of frustration, or making fun of what is being said, will stop you from hearing the real message.

As Speakers

Use negative words, expressions, and body language also creates misinterpretation and discourages good listening. It is necessary, when speaking, to use positive (or neutral) words, phrases, and body language to attract open and attentive listeners.

Habits to Promote Good Listening Direct Self-expression Often believe that their partner understands their desires, thoughts, and views even though they have never been verbalized. Far too often, that's just not the case: expecting your partner to be able to read your mindsets both of you up for negative results — pain, frustration, misunderstandings. Do you want to avoid this can miscommunication? If so, the answer is simple: make your feelings as straightforward, truthful, and optimistic as you can. Don't stop thinking about it because you're afraid of what your partner is going to think about. Reflect on how it is going to influence you. Seek not to blame or judge your friend when you're voicing yourself. Don't use sentences like "Unlike you, I ..." or "It's because of you that ... "—these comments would weaken every attempt to interact well.

Using "I" Messages

An efficient way to connect with your partner is through "I" messages — statements that explain your emotions and tell you how your partner's actions affect you. "I" messages should convey emotions in a way that is not intrusive, as they focus on the thoughts of the speaker and do not blame the listener.

"I" messages vary so much from a "you" message. "You" messages accuse the other person and judge him based on their behavior. "You" messages also activate your partner's defensiveness or aggression and appear to heighten conflict. Think of how you felt while listening to "You always ..." or "You never ..."

The Mechanics of "I" Messages

"I" messages let your partner know what you feel about it and why you feel like that. "I" has three pieces to the messages: 1. A comment on the feelings of a speaker 2. Statement of conduct that triggered sensation 3. The explanation for the feeling of the speaker

Practice Using "I" Statements

"I get angry whenever you criticize my parents because they are so dear to me." This 'I' statement follows the three steps we mentioned: it describes the feeling: 'I get upset' It describes the behavior: 'when you criticize my parents' It explains the reason: 'because my parents are so important to me.'

Different Communication Styles

Communication, as mentioned earlier, plays a very important part in satisfying partners in marriage.

If you'd like better contact with your partner, knowing some of the variations in communication styles is a positive thing.

Expressive

One partner is theoretically more vocal. Expressive people tend to express their thoughts and feelings. They are looking for feedback or answers in real-time.

Task- or Fact-oriented
Another partner may rarely speak about feelings, and will use facts rather than emotions, as in: "I feel I'm not making enough money." This person seeks approval of his / her point of view, not emotions.

When Opposites Attract
Both opposite styles may initially attract each other — and they may have trouble dealing with what's going on in the relationship over time as the relationship becomes more complicated.

Getting to the Heart of the Matter
Trying to understand the communication style of each other and reacting accordingly is crucial. To do this, couples should know

that contact is without secrets. You get better by doing, learning, learning. Communicating knowledge of our inner lives is a crucial aspect of an intimate relationship. At this point, talking and listening is a way to feel connected.

Practicing and learning New Habits
Successful communication is not easy

Teaching and learning new communication skills requires persistence, persistence, patience, and practice. It's important to take the time to converse. Your relationship offers a safe place for expressing your emotions, thoughts, fears, dreams, and hopes. Make a concerted effort to make time for more regular conversations with your partner.

In challenging times, people feel frustrated by problems and obligations.

Time together as a couple is always the last thing on our minds, as we struggle with daily life's hassles. Although you may be distracted, exhausted, and concerned, take the time to reflect on the needs of your partners and spend uninterrupted, quality time together. Even thinking about what has happened a few minutes a day can be a relief from tension. When you and your partner are not exhausted or disturbed, ask that these complicated or problem- conversations should be reserved for other times.

You will need to be the conversation starter

Having the one who initiates discussions is worth the effort. When you are sensitive to changes in the emotions and needs of your partner, you will find several ways to open the door to communication.

If in a relationship, you need to develop communication skills, you can feel like a major, daunting challenge. Yet it's one that needs to happen, as it enhances every aspect of your relationship. "Dialogue is undeniably the most important skill in any relationship," says Dr. Michele Kerulis, Therapy Specialist and Professor for Connections and Dating @ Northwestern to Bustle. "Communication allows us to voice our basic needs to others and also provides opportunities to approach topics like sex and romance, stress management, and conflict resolution."

Communication is crucial to a relationship — but it's also a really easy thing to tweak. So, don't be stressed if you feel like you're not communicating properly. Because the thing about communication that we need to have in mind is that it's the little things that make a lasting difference. Yes, it's really important to be able to not agree and fight well. In fact, being able to fight in a compassionate way can save a relationship. But if your daily communication skills are on point, then actually those big conversations aren't so scary. Because you know you have the skills to reach each other, and you do it before any issue gets out of control. So, focus on the day-to-day things. Here are little ways you can make your communication skills a lot better:

1. Ask How They Are Daily

Check-in every day. Asking "How are you? How was your day?" will not only keep you in touch and in sync, it'll help keep you in the habit of communicating with each other.

2. Never Assume

It's easy to get worked up in your own head about something, but never actually reach out to the other person. "Assumptions and mind-reading usually lead to misunderstandings and hurt feelings," Sameera Sullivan, psychologist and founder of Lasting Connections, tells Bustle. Never assume you know what they're thinking—reach out instead.

3. **Listen, Listen, Listen**

Communication is about not just talking; but also, about being an active listener. Who is an active listener? "[They] listen to what their partner says, instead of being defensive without knowing the partner's point of view or where they come from, "says Janet Zinn, a couple of therapists based in New York City, to Bustle.

4. **Don't Nitpick**

Little digs can build up. If you have a problem, say it. Don't make little commends — they're immature, and they will slowly corrode your relationship.

5. **Have Regular Relationship Check-Ins**

Just like you should ask how they are every day; you need to check in about the big stuff too. Make sure that you ask, "How do you feel about us?" and if there are any big changes — moving in, getting engaged, going on a summer break— be sure to talk about them regularly. It gives the both of you an important platform to air concerns.

6. **Believe Things Can Change**

Part of having a positive conversation and communication is having a positive attitude. Don't approach problems as though they're impossible to solve.

7. **Respond**

If your partner is reaching out to you, be there to meet them. "Couples try to catch each other's attention all day long, whether it's for encouragement, talk, attraction, play, validation, feeling linked or love. "Each of these moments is a chance to communicate with your partner. A person should look for someone who listens to them, or at least acknowledge them when they try to get their attention, as it means they are fulfilling your emotional needs — or at least attempting to do so."

Whether it's just talking about their day or trying to discuss big issues, recognize that they're reaching out and meet them.

8. **Talk Things Through Before They Happen**

If you know you have a stressful time coming up, touch base beforehand. When I had family stress, I said to my partner, "This is happening. I'm sorry if I'm a little all over the place for the next week or two."

That way, not only did she know it wasn't her, we had something to refer back to when I was feeling stressed and needed to talk about it.

9. **Say "Thank You"**

"A perfect way to create trust is to show appreciation for something your partner has thoughtfully done that day," Bustle tells Samantha Burns, relationship counselor, and dating coach. So quick.

10. **Discuss Your Sexual Fantasies**

Being able to talk about sex openly doesn't just mean you'll both be more satisfied. It shows a real connection. "In my experience, partners who talk openly about their fantasies tend to have good communication, solid trust, and more excitement, which leads to great sex and nourishing relationships," sexologist and relationship therapist, Kelly McDonnell-Arnold, tells Bustle

11. **And Communicate During Sex**

You don't need to be into dirty talk to communicate during sex. Giving verbal cues is great, but moaning, leading their hands, even just saying what feels good are all great ways to make sure that the communication is happening in all areas of your relationship — bedroom included.

12. **Use Feeling Language**

I'm logical. So logical that, in times of stress, it can appear a bit dispassionate. It's not dispassionate — I'm feeling a lot— but it doesn't come across. If you're like me, try to focus on feeling language. Talk about how you're feeling and affected by things. It's done wonders for me.

13. **Pick Your Timing**

So often we bring something up when we're feeling frustrated or annoyed. But pick your timing. Don't bring up a big problem if there's no time to discuss it properly. Don't approach your partner with a bunch of small problems while stressing about something big. You'll know when it's a good time.

14. **Take the Time To Compliment Each Other**

If you get too comfortable with each other, it's easy to only bring things up if they're bothering you. You start to get complacent about the good things and take them for granted, which can breed resentment. Keep pointing out what you appreciate and love about each other.

15. **Never Stop Flirting**

Communication doesn't all have to be serious; in fact, keeping up the way you flirted when you first met is important to your relationship. "Couples who stop flirting are couples who stop anticipating," Certified relationship coach Chris Armstrong tells Bustle. "Things go blasé, and what was once an unpredictable stroll is now an expected lull." Don't lose that first flirty feeling.

It might feel like communication is all about those very big and deep discussions. But in reality, it's all about maintaining the little things. Having a strong foundation will put you in a much better position for those tricky talks.

Effective contact should be part of any healthy partnership, tips for Good Contact Open. Using the instructions below to open communication channels between your partner and yourself. When you are present in a nonhealthy or toxic relationship, use those tips carefully. You know best about your relationship. If any of those tips put you at risk, don't pursue them.

Seek to: Find the Right Time for better contact

When you are disturbed by something, and you would like to have a chat about it, choosing the right time to speak may be helpful. Consider finding a moment when you and your partner are relaxed, not upset, anxious, or in a rush. If one or both of you is very busy, you might even suggest scheduling a time to chat!

Face to Face Chat

Stop speaking in writing about sensitive matters or questions. You may misunderstand the text messages, letters, and emails. Chat in person, and no needless miscommunications arise. When you have difficulty gathering your thoughts, try writing them down in advance to your friend and reading them out loud.

Should not wrestle

Even if we mean well, because of our word choice, we can often come off as harsh. Saying "you" can sound as if you're bullying, making your partner defensive and less open to your message. Instead, try to use "I" or "we." Say, for instance, "I feel like we haven't been so close lately" instead of "You've been distant with me."

Agree on being frank. Honesty hurts sometimes, but that is the secret to a healthy relationship. Admit that when you make a mistake instead of making excuses, you're not always flawless and apologize. You'll feel happier, and that's going to help improve the friendship.

Practice the language of the body

Let your partner know that you are listening to them with your full attention: sit down, face them, and make eye contact as they talk. Do not take a phone call, write a text, or play a video game while you talk. By listening and answering, show your partner that you appreciate them.

Using the Law of 48 Hours

If your partner is doing something that makes you upset, you'll need to tell them. But you just don't have to do it instantly. If 48 hours later, you are still hurt, then say something. If not, then think about it forgetting. Yet note that your friend will not be able to read your mind. When you're not talking up when you're angry, so there's no way they can apologize or alter. When you mention your hurt feelings and genuinely apologize to your partner, let it go. If they aren't important, don't bring up past issues.

CHAPTER 14 - HOW TO COMMUNICATE IF YOU ARE ANGRY

It's all right to get upset in a relationship at some point; everyone is doing it!

What is crucial is that you do a safe way of resolving disputes. If you get upset with your friend, you have to take a few steps here:

Stop it

Pause, take a step back, and relax if you get really upset about something. Tell your partner that you'd like to have a short break prior to the commencement of the conversation. Allow yourself the opportunity to calm down by watching TV, talking to a friend, playing a video game, walking, listening to some music, or something that allows you to relax. Having a break will help prevent things from getting worse.

Just remember

Think about the situation when you're not agitated any more, and why you got so mad. Is it like your friend is talking, or they did something? Then think about ways of explaining how you feel and figure out the real problem.

Speech

Eventually, discuss with your partner and follow the guidelines above when you do.

Hear

Remember to stop talking after you tell your partner how you feel and listen to what they have to say. You also deserve a chance to share your feelings in a comfortable and secure atmosphere.

Communication is not always straightforward. Many of these tips can sound uncomfortable or awkward at first, but they will help you better connect and develop a healthier relationship.

Understanding Couple Conflict:

Only imagine you've only bought a brand-new vehicle. It's your dream car, the one you've been dreaming for so many years, and you've finally bought it! You leave it to go to work in the parking lot and find a SCRATCH when you get out. How would you react?

You may be jumping and crying, tearing your hair out, being completely mad that someone had the audacity to hit your car. You do some work and find that if you take the time and energy to do it, you can carefully buff the scratch-off. So, you're cleaning the surface where the scratch is, polishing the area, then cleaning it once more using an expensive solvent to clean waxes and oils prior to painting.

A week or two goes by, and when you go inside, you leave the car parked in the grocery store lot. You come out, and what are you going to find? A DENT on the bumper behind you! You are riled up really now. Has a DENT in your brand-new vehicle, the one you just spent what feels like a lifetime to patch a scratch on.

You go to a specialist this time to fix the issue. It takes a number of days and a lot of work, but now the scratch is practically invisible. Another near phone call!

Yet when you have your sixth or seventh scratch, what does happen? You don't bother buffing out those marks anymore because any time there's a little ding, you can't just take the car in for bodywork. You start letting go of it, and you stop caring at some point. What cares if a scratch is on the car? He also has six new ones. Right?

And what if we don't talk about your car. What if your relationship is discussed?

Tony Robbins' approach to relationships

This is because they are fortunate, extraordinarily well suited, entirely incompatible, or submerged in great chemistry that genuinely exceptional and productive relationships don't touch people. Extraordinary, caring, long-lasting, stable relationships are the results of the love laws of hard work, commitment, and practice. Knowing how to never doubt your partner's purpose, taking the time to understand what makes them special and wonderful, and discovering ways to disrupt negative or repetitive behaviors in fun and fascinating ways are only three of the laws that will help you develop an exceptional relationship.

Through 10 disciplines of love and passion, there are seven master skills we can learn, practice, refine, and apply. Such master skills and disciplines are key to Tony's approach to advice on relationships, and – spoiler warning! – They operate, regardless of who you are or at what stage of your relationship. Through harnessing the power of skills such as granting your partner independence and accepting unconditional love and compassion, you are opening the door to a relationship that is more rewarding than you would ever imagine. Imagine living with someone who is your number one fan and your best friend and loving them. If you follow the relationship guide of Tony Robbins, you might have that kind of relationship.

Most people in a relationship rely too much on what to look for. Know that you first need to focus on yourself before you can build the healthy relationship you want. The trick is living as your genuine self, in charge of your anxiety. If you increase the expectations that you hold to, not only do you raise the standards of your partnership, but you will also help your partner bring out the best. You can often be attributed to being furious, sad, or jealous in a relationship, rather than your partner.

You will find in this relationship guide tools to discover and analyze the secrets of relationship success that will lead you to the satisfying relationship that you have always desired. You will learn to cultivate the passion and happiness you share with the person you love or to recognize what you want in your next relationship and what has stopped you from finding the satisfaction you deserve. You'll cultivate the potential to establish and maintain a safe, respectful, long-lasting relationship that appeals to your core values and expectations.

You'll also learn the resources you need to lead you and your relationship through the most difficult times, helping you and your partner deal with feelings of anxiety, tension, and confusion. Rather than being right, you should learn to concentrate on being caring and accommodating and to also realize that it is when your partner is the most uncooperative or distant, they need your love most.

You'll also learn how to rekindle a romantic, exceptional relationship in this revolutionary relationship guide, how to cope with difficulties that eventually arise, and how to nurture and maintain your relationship for continuous growth and ultimate joy and fulfillment. You will be reassured that stability is at the heart of a successful relationship and how you could take your relationship to new heights by letting go of commitment and the desire for good. You'll also know when not to be flexible, and when undermining your core values in a relationship.

Are you willing to take action and build a satisfying relationship that gives the rest of your life a supporting structure?

THE BASICS:

The Secret to Communication in Relationships

What are the discrepancies between simple knowledge exchange and deep, integrated levels of healthy relationship contact? Learn how good communication can be practiced by aligning core principles for you and your family.

Rekindle your relationship's passion

Learn how to bring love back into your relationship. You must define approaches to overcome the problems that your partnership will bring down if you don't use them as opportunities to move it to the next stage.

How to overcome conflict and save the relationship.

Consider two couples: one that uses conflict to develop their relationship and one that uses conflict to integrate it into their relationship, and etch it. Which one do you think would bring about fulfillment? In a stable partnership, learn how to use disagreements to develop.

You deserve to forge the right relationship

What does a healthy relationship look like and feel like? Read about the positive force of polarity and how to create trust with the one you love by demonstrating that even in the toughest of times, you can fulfill their core human needs.

Overcome the insecurities in your relationship

Find ways to stop feelings of anxiety that could disrupt your relationship. Fight any romantic vulnerability and establish the enduring, safe relationship you deserve.

Signs of a romantic relationship Do you have an intimate and caring relationship with your partner? Below are the ten signs of a truly passionate connection.

Dive Deeper: Core Concepts

The ten guiding principles of an exceptional connection Your partnership can only be as good as the expectations you set for it. When you have poor expectations, then you will have a partnership of low quality. They provide your own set of standards. Tell yourself, how good am I with a partner? You start with a good and loving relationship and the appreciation you feel for being with the one you love.

Will you want to be a fantastic partner? Follow the ten guiding principles of an excellent partnership and practice it.

The # 1 rule of attraction: polarity

The love in your relationship has to do with your partner's strength, and vice versa. The more the efforts opposed, the more attraction there is, just as there is more pull between the magnets. This principle is known as polarity, and if the polarity fades with time in your relationship, then love does so.

You can almost instantly change the level of attraction in your relationship, like a switch flip. Read about polarity and why a perfect relationship is essential to accepting it.

The five stressors of the relationship

Do you know what you will do when you first meet your partner? Virtually nothing, right? How and why burns out this fire, this sparkle? None of us see that coming; it's all ramping upon us. One day we find that passion and desire are gone. The reality is there's a depolarization cycle leading to other signs such as anger and a lack of commitment. That doesn't have to be like this.

You have the ability to alter destiny. If you understand the five core stressors of the relationship, then you will have the know-how to restore its magic.

You will describe the relationships by your degree of commitment. Was it all about you, or do you split the job in equal measure? Or, are you completely devoted to one another and your partner? The quality of a partner and that of a partnership can be determined by the manner in which you have a world-centered view. Do you care deeply about the needs of your family or even yourselves?

Improvement starts with you. If you are sincerely committed to reigniting the fire in your relationship, see how successful you are as a partner.

The ultimate measure of relationship

A good relationship is based on honesty and trust, which begins with honest with yourself. Where do you stand in your relationship? Are you enamored head-over-heels? And, ready for running? Now, ask yourself: Where will you be? You will build the relationship of your dreams if you are true to yourself and know where you are and have confidence about where you want to go.

Where is your relationship? Be true to yourself and be transparent.

One thing is easy to forget in today's world of dating reality shows, mobile apps, and romantic comedies: relationships are work. We never "swipe right," fall in love and live happily ever after automatically. And when things get rough, it's easy to throw in the towel, say "it wouldn't have worked out anyway," and move on – instead of doing the research to learn how to save a relationship.

But it's worth saving your friendship.

You've got the history. You have been through a lot of things together – a lot of relationships last years or even decades before you got to this level. Your partner knows you more than anyone else, and like no one else will, they'll be there for you. Seek these nine tips on how to save your relationship before you lose all hope.

You're still reading about how to save your relationship, so you found out the first step: you've got to want to save it. If there's that drive, you need to learn how to turn it into positive measures that can repair what's broken, overcome underlying issues and eventually save your relationship.

How destructive is conflict? A dispute with your significant other could make you feel assaulted or threatened, helpless, and powerless, which can make you recoil and withdraw. For things that annoy your partner and you feel you're under attack, you're less likely to react constructively and more likely to turn to old standbys such as "the silent treatment," which actually does more damage than good. In the end, this will cause your relationship to completely break down.

If someone asked you if you knew how to resolve conflict, you'd probably say yes, and if they asked you if the silent treatment was a good way to deal with conflict, you'd almost definitely say no. You know better than resorting to such dumb tactics, but you do it anyway if you're hurt enough. Why? For what? Why return to negative habits instead of actively trying to correct the communication problems at hand?

1. Examine your attention.

A dispute is dangerous when you focus on protecting yourself from attack rather than problem-solving. By concentrating on the pain and discomfort, you're making sure you're going to experience more of the same, and where the emphasis goes, energy flows, or as Tony notes, "What we're always focused on is exactly what we're going to experience in our lives." Tony will take a two-lane highway at 10–20-yard intervals supported by power line posts. Many of these appeared to be roses, candles, and photos constantly decorating him. With so much room on either side of the post, it was surprising how many people reaching it had died or been injured. Why didn't the perpetrator get away with it? Why were they not swerving to either side?

This is so people should focus all their energy not to reach the pole. Nevertheless, our priority is setting our course. If we don't want to reach the pole, we have to focus on what we want to do: stay on the lane! Through changing our attention, we can change the result.

This lesson discusses how you can save your relationship. If you concentrate on where you don't want your relationship to end, struggle and let frustration build up over, you'll find yourself where you don't want to be – either in a miserable, unfulfilling relationship or split completely from your partner. If you concentrate on dispute resolution and evolving together, you will get the results you want.

2. Communicate

You're passing time in a coffee shop and there are two couples seated near you in the store. The couple to your left are debating with friends about whether they want to go to dinner. He says, "It's never pleasant – you said so yourself last time." She responds, "Of course you'd say that, because they're my friends, and you've never given any of my friends a chance." He rolls his eyes, and in a rather cynical tone, he says, "We're going here. War and Peace, our personal version, volume whatever." They turn away and sit in silence.

The people to your right are still thinking about how they want to have dinner with friends. He says, "I think I'm a little worried that it's going to go on for hours and that it may not be that fun. What do you think?" She asks, "I get that. I really want to go, but probably we should arrange a time when we're going to have to quit as a compromise?" She goes on, squeezing his hand and laughing, "Plus, it's going to be nice to get home early."

Both pairs were faced with a conflict-in fact the same conflict. Yet, in one relationship, one knew how to settle the conflict, and the other did not. One responded by relying on bad habits and using a gap between them to expand the dispute. The other has used the dispute as an opportunity to express their feelings and to improve their relationship. Which pair do you think the partnership is more fruitful and fulfilling? -- partnership do you expect to last longer? Communication on how to save a relationship is at the top of the list.

3. **Turn conflict into opportunity**.

In the example of a coffee shop, a couple has figured out how to overcome conflict in a relationship: don't become defensive; don't pound your point; don't try to fight. How would you have wanted to lose your friend, the one you love? You will let go of petty arguments and support positive contact when you agree that there are no losers in life.

Conflicts give you and your partner the ability to agree with principles and results. Chances of recognizing, appreciating, and accepting differences are they. Put yourself in the role of your friend, and try to understand his or her experience. Such interactions and feelings can be painful, but we will never develop if we just opt for comfort.

Conflict is also an opportunity to know more about your partner and to appreciate them even more. Prepare to see disagreements as changes to something greater than as grounds for retreating. The next time you disagree with your significant other and question how to save your relationship, try to see the good in the situation rather than the negative and resolve actively to work together for a more prosperous future.

4. Using humor

If you in one way or the other, find yourself in a ring of revenge, use humor to break the trend is a successful tactic. Humor will relieve stress and encourage you and your partner to concentrate on what you really want – learning how to rescue your relationship – and not on what you don't want, another needless fight.

When you sense an argument is escalating, take a moment to interrupt the debate. Consider acting as Christopher Walken or William Shatner would argue. Sing a song that will make your partner laugh. Consider the argument absurd.

Let's go back to the coffee shop example to illustrate this point. You see the older set. Accidentally, the man spills his tea across the table and splashes on the favorite dress of his friend. He gets up to get some napkins, and she laughs and shouts out to the other customers, "He's been doing this to me for twenty years – he's never finished a cup yet!" He comes back, cleans the tea off her, and then shouts back to the other customers, "She's been waiting for it!" They all laugh, and you and everyone else in the shop, too.

Many people may have converted the situation into an argument, but this husband

and wife embraced the moment by using humor to nip the retaliatory cycle in the bud and converted it into an opportunity to learn how to overcome tension in a relationship.

5. **Ask the right questions**

If you're thinking of how a relationship can be saved, chances are things have gone wrong for quite some time. Not only do you need to dig into the past to discover the true, deeper problems, but look to the future too. Everything it's about asking the right questions about yourself.

Next, make sure that you start the exercise from the right perspective. The point is not to criticize, dig up old grievances, or tell your partner all the irritating things they do. You have to change your way of thinking to one of appreciation and acceptance. Focus on the fact that life is happening to you, not to you. Only the present state of your relationship gives you the ability to learn and develop – as long as you're open to what it has to teach you.

Now you're able to ask important questions about yourself: Why did your relationship break down? These are the limiting values that shaped your relationship that you and your partner lived through? Why do you win them over? So, what is it that you want for the future? What do you concentrate on in your relationship?

6. Exercise acceptance

Extend your current outlook on abundance to your partner. Many of our partners do things that bother us or have behaviors, and no human being is flawless. Reflect more on what they bring to the table, how they make you feel and the things you value, instead of focusing on their negative characteristics or bad habits. You'll find that you'll soon start loving all the things that used to make you nuts because they're part of the whole person you love, your partner.

Remember the two in-café couples? The popular couple, who put effort into knowing each other's needs, reaffirmed their mutual support – they supported his need to leave at a certain hour, and they supported her need to socialize with friends. They consulted with each other, evaluated the needs of each other, and made it a fun problem to solve, rather than making anything small turn into a big argument.

Hear your friend and hear what they're doing and why they act the way they're doing. Then always embrace yourself: be frank about your own emotions and feelings. Be your bona fide self. Personal failures shouldn't be the reason you're wondering how to save your relationship. Yes, they are a strong device to show your partner how much you love them.

7. A confrontation with your partner can make you feel insulted or threatened, helpless and fragile, and that can make you recoil and withdraw. When you feel like you are under siege, you are less likely to react constructively, and more likely to return to old standbys such as "the silent treatment," which actually does more harm than good. In the end, this will cause your relationship to completely break down.

If someone asked you if you knew how to fix the conflict, you would probably say yes, and if they asked you if the silent treatment was a good way to deal with conflict, you would almost definitely say no. You know better than resorting to such dumb tactics, but you do it anyway if you're hurt enough. Why? For what? Why return to negative habits instead of actively trying to correct the communication problems at hand?

Break the cycle of aggression and give positive energy to the conflict. Do not become defensive; do not pound your point; try not to win. How would you have wanted to lose your friend, the one you love?

8. Work on forgiveness.

You're probably feeling furious, bitter, hurt, mistrustful, and a whole host of other negative emotions if you're wondering how to save your relationship because your confidence broke. You feel guilty and embarrassed when you are the one who broke the trust. You may also want to blame your partner for your acts or justify them. Both spouses need to focus on a pardon in this case.

One day you're not only going to wake up and start magically forgiving your mate. Pardoning is a method. It's a series of small acts that add up over time-admitting mistakes, practicing absolute honesty, and putting your partner first. Pardoning requires time.

If you're the one who lost the faith, you have to take full responsibility. Respect your partner's way of harming them, and give them the space they deserve. First, bring your partner in, and don't fall into a self-blame trap. If your faith has been breached, take some space but keep on talking. Let your partner know what the trust you need to restore. Above everything, never give up.

9. Allow time for touch

When you're constantly arguing with your partner when you're irritated with any little thing they do - it can be hard to be affectionate. But you've got to give time to reach. This does not only mean sex – but it also means cuddling during a movie on the sofa, stealing a morning kiss before work, and holding hands for no reason whatsoever.

There is a reason why loving your partner makes you feel so good: cuddling, kissing, and even holding your hands triggers oxytocin to be released, a "feel-good" chemical in your brain that make you feel protected and secure. Oxytocin will help you feel more linked to your partner and even decrease blood pressure. You are having all those advantages only by reaching out and taking the hand of your friend.

Should not withhold physical contact-even when you are insane-or, you can find yourself in a marriage that is totally sexless. If you really want your relationship saved, start with physical contact. Cuddle in before going to bed. Hold hands with friends when you're out for dinner. Sneak up a kiss when you're eating. A good relationship is not a product of physical intimacy – it produces a happy relationship.

Relationships aren't easy. We are all imperfect-so errors are made by humans. We also have shortcomings. Occasionally we're just not putting in the effort we need and letting our relationships slip by the way. It may have been overlooked for years by the time we start looking at how to save a relationship. Yet remember: There are plenty of partnerships worth saving. You just have to be able to do the job.

Consider the four stages of marital conflict and save your marriage partnership.

Throughout their novel The Seven Conflicts, authors Tim and Joy Downs say the couple who never learn how to deal with their conflicts effectively begin a sequence of phases that can inevitably kill them.

What is marital dispute?

Marital dispute is not a pure difference of opinion. Rather, it is a sequence of incidents that were treated badly in order to seriously harm the marital relationship. Issues of marriage have festered to the point where stubbornness, pride, resentment, hurt, and animosity hinder successful communication of marriage.

Nearly all serious marital discord has its origin in selfishness on the part of one or both parties. Saving a marriage requires denying selfishness, giving up ego, forgiving hurt, and putting aside bitterness; these steps are becoming more difficult, so it is best to stop the spiraling downward of marital conflict.

Preventing marital conflict is the best way of doing marriage work. Preparation for marriage is accompanied by premarital therapy. If that doesn't happen, then immediately after the wedding, marriage relationship therapy will provide couples simple marital dispute resolution techniques that can be used before marriage issues get out of control.

Marriage is a partnership in which trust is developed over time, as devoted partners set aside their own desires for the good of their partner and build skills to sustain a healthy and open relationship.

Who gives rise to marital conflict?

As mentioned above, egoism is the key cause of disputes over marriage. Another way to mean this is that marital problems arise when one party thinks it has its way. While one has personal interests, a choice that often affects the marriage is to demand that one's self-interest prevail. Could any relationship succeed if one party constantly gets his or her way? Clearly not.

If the marriage partnership is to succeed, then giving up self-interest is something to which couples have to become accustomed. Sacrifice finally is a pleasure and not a burden.

But it's not just giving in and never getting your way. The marriage partnership grows deeper as partners lovingly share and explore their desires, often displaying a willingness to compromise while working together genuinely to mutually possess the best marriage solution.

How marital conflict impacts marriage relationships If husbands and wives are unable to resolve their conflicts, as indicated by the four stages of marital conflict, they collapse into repetitive conduct patterns. Recognizing that all these stages are unstable, is significant. The stage of negotiation and agreement may appear promising, but it will disintegrate without commitment and a clear understanding of the challenges and obstacles that have to be addressed.

When correspondence about marriage breaks down, feelings get hurt, emotions run high, and solutions seem out of control. The harm multiplies when marital disputes and children are living in the same household.

Four levels of marital dispute in which marital discord increases:

1. Have It Your Way.

Couples newly married and unable to overcome their differences correctly prefer to seek to settle problems by avoiding conflict. Without ever resolving the core problem, they cede together. If you fight against your husband, you will slowly find yourself uncomfortable about it and start to change your attitude to the next point.

2. Have It My Way.

When couples have drained themselves by ignoring their own needs, they often transform the opposite way and begin insisting that their needs are now met. A wife who has held her feelings to herself will suddenly realize that this has led to her suffering and may start expressing her thoughts and attitudes at every opportunity. Yet sadly, this stage doesn't work either as husband and wife begin butting heads.

3. Have It Our Way.

The third phase involves compromising and bargaining with each other. The pair may initially be excited about their new communication style, but the excitement fades slowly. For a marriage at this time, partners face more time constraints and stresses from their parenting, financial problems, and hectic schedules. Between an unsuccessful conflict resolution style and the can pressures of life, couples can start to doubt their relationship during this time.

4. **Have It the Way You Like.**

This stage represents a sense of resignation. Couples at this point are overwhelmed by the constant disputes, and may even feel discouraged that all the unresolved issues will ever be resolved. If you are at this point, then you need expert guidance on marriage.

Good Marital Communication

Marriages due to disagreement should not have to end up this way. Couples should work through their problems with good communication and dispute management skills, rather than ignoring or dragging out the issues. Begin finding new ways to interact with your husband if you identify one of these unpleasant phases of your own marriage. If you're unsure where to start, check out the library for a few books, read articles online, or talk with the popular couples you know. Try attending a marriage therapist to help teach you constructive approaches if conflict appears to go unresolved.

Conflict is a routine feature of almost all ties. This can be a significant source of tension, too. Hence it is important to find a resolution with most conflicts. It sounds like a simple assumption, but sometimes people are suppressing their frustration or only 'going along to get along.' Others believe they are causing one by resolving a dispute and just staying silent when upset.

It is, unfortunately, not a balanced long-term approach.

Unresolved conflict within the partnership may lead to frustration and additional unresolved conflict.

But more critically, continuing conflict can potentially have a detrimental effect on your wellbeing and life. Sadly, conflict resolution can also be difficult. In reality, attempts at conflict resolution, done poorly, may make the conflict worse.

Researcher John Gottman and his colleagues, for example, have been researching how couples compete, and can actually predict which couples will go on to divorce by analyzing their dispute solving skills — or lack of them.

(Hint: Couples who are constantly criticizing their partner's character, or shutting down during arguments rather than working through conflict in a proactive, respectful way, should watch out.) For those who weren't born into a family where perfect conflict resolution skills were modeled on a daily basis (and—let's face it—how many of us were?), here are some guidelines to make conflict resolution more simple and less stressful.

Get in Touch With Your Feelings

Just you are interested in an essential aspect of dispute resolution — knowing how you feel and why you feel so. Your feelings may seem clear to you now, but this isn't always the case. You feel upset or resentful at times but don't know why. Many times, you believe the other person doesn't do what they 'should' do, yet you don't know precisely what you expect from them, or whether it's even sensible.

Journaling can be an important way to get in contact with your own emotions, opinions, and desires so you can express them to the other person more effectively. This cycle often brings up some pretty heavy issues, and psychotherapy can be helpful.

Using Journaling

Hone Your Listening Skills

How effectively we listen is at least as critical when it comes to successful conflict resolution as to how effectively we express ourselves. If we are to come to a conclusion, it is important to consider the viewpoint of the other person, rather than just our own. In reality, actually making the other person feel heard and understood can often go a long way towards a conflict resolution. Effective listening also helps you close the distance between the two of you, realize where the difference is, and so on.

Sadly, active listening has not been acknowledged by anyone and it's normal for people to believe they're listening, when they're just formulating their next answer in their minds, thinking to themselves how wrong the other person is, or doing something other than trying to consider the viewpoint of the other person. It's also normal in your own viewpoint to be so protective and stubborn that you can't simply hear the other person's point of view.

Practice Assertive Communication

Communicating your thoughts and desires clearly is also a vital part of conflict resolution. As you already know, saying the wrong thing can be like throwing gasoline on a fire and making a dispute worse. The key thing to note is to express what's on your mind in a way that is straightforward and assertive, without being offensive or putting the other person on the defensive.

One successful dispute management technique is to put it in terms of how you feel rather than what you believe the other person is doing wrong, using 'I feel' comments.

5 Quick Steps to Assertive Communication

Seek a Resolution

Once you understand the other person's viewpoint, and they understand yours, it's time to find a resolution to the conflict — a resolution you all can live with. Occasionally a clear and logical response pops up because both sides understand the other person's perspective. For situations where the dispute was focused on a misunderstanding or a lack of perspective to the other's point of view, a clear explanation can work well, and an open dialogue can bring people back together.

Other times, there is a little more research needed. For situations where there's a disagreement about an issue and both parties don't agree, you have a few options: Sometimes you may or may not agree, sometimes you may find a compromise or middle ground, and in some situations, the individual who feels more strongly about an issue can get their way, with the agreement that they will negotiate the next time. The main thing is to come to a position of compromise and seek and sort it out in a way that's respectful of those involved.

Know When It's Not Working

Because of the cost that continuing conflict can extract on an individual, sometimes it's best to put some distance in the relationship or break ties completely.1 In cases of violence, basic dispute resolution strategies can only take you so far, so personal protection needs to take precedence.

If coping with challenging family members, on the other hand, adding a few limits and respecting the other person's weaknesses in the relationship will bring some harmony. In partnerships that are unsupportive or marked by ongoing conflict, letting go can be a great source of stress relief. Only you can determine whether a relationship can be strengthened, or should be let go Drawing from over four decades of research results, we have been able to categorize couples into five types: Conflict-Avoiding, Validating, Contentious, Aggressive, and Aggressive-Detached.

The three happy couple styles (Conflict-Avoiding, Validating, and Volatile) come from Harold Raush's seminal book Communication, Conflict, and Marriage, in which Raush analyzes relationships between spouses to distinguish happily from unhappily married couples. Each relationship is very special, and every relationship of couple has its benefits and risks.

Of the two unhappy couple styles we have been able to classify in the Love Lab, Hostile couples remained unhappily married, while Hostile-Detached couples eventually divorced.

Do you know what kind you are?

1. **Conflict avoiders**

Conflict avoiders eliminate attempts at persuasion and stress their common ground areas instead. They avoid confrontation, avoid voicing what they need from each other, and praise their relationship for being content in general. In the balance between freedom and interdependence, an important thing of pairs avoiding conflict is. We have strong boundaries and are people with different interests.

It is not meant to denigrate the nature of the places they visit and rely on each other. For those areas of overlap where they are interdependent, they may be very related and loving. Although they are minimally expressive in terms of sentiment, they possess a positive-to-negative effect ratio of about five to one. Their weighting of SPAFF (Specific Affect Coding System) is not overwhelmingly optimistic, but it is not at all bad. Their engagement is to them nice enough.

2. **Volatile Couples**

In fact, volatile couples are intensely emotional, almost the exact opposite of conflict avoiders. They immediately begin persuasion during a confrontational discussion and stick to it during the discussion. Their conversation is marked by a lot of laughter, mutual fun, and humor. We seem to enjoy debating and arguing but are not rude and hostile.

Their ratio positive-negative? Five to one.

Whereas there may be many articulated adverse consequences, including frustration and feelings of fear, but no disdain. They don't have good boundaries across their individual worlds, and the overlap is massive. While they have to debate much about their positions, their contact emphasizes interaction and integrity.

3. **Validating Couples**

These couples 'relationships are marked by comfort and calmness. They're sort of vocal but mostly quiet. They seem to be intermediate in several respects between the evaders and the explosive couples. They put great importance on accepting and respecting the point of view of their partner, and are also empathetic about the feelings of their partner.

We will face their disagreements, but only on some subjects and not on others. On certain things, they can become highly competitive and can turn into a power struggle. Normally, instead, they settle down and negotiate. Validating partners are only slightly vocal in terms of emotion during the conflict. The positive-to-negative impact ratio for validators once again was around five to one.

4. **Aggressive Couples**

Aggressive couples are like validating couples, except that both spouses have high degrees of defensiveness. In Love Lab research with heterosexual couples, the husband was generally the validator, and the avoider was the wife. That was based on shapes of influence feature that you can learn more about in Principia Amoris: The New Love Study.

There was also a lot of blame, assertions of "you still" and "you never" and complaining. During the confrontation, each partner expressed their own viewpoint, and no support or appreciation for either person's point of view existed between partners. There was plenty of scorn. Each Four Horsemen was there.

5. Such couples are like two armies engaged in a mutually exhausting and lonely standoff with no definite victor, only a stalemate. During the confrontation, they snipe at each other, but the air is full of emotional detachment and indifference, like gun smoke.

We noticed in the Love Lab that escalating conflict between two validators would arise, but then one of them is going back down. But the unpredictable one will let the validator withdraw? Definitely not.

So, why ends up divorcing the violently separated couple? Why is the pair not hostile? May it be that the response is linked to the second phase of love, the period of "establishing confidence?" Our love equations have an explanation: Aggressive (validator-avoider) couples control their negativity, whereas aggressive (validator-volatile) couples do not control their negativity.

Conflict in relationships

What Kevin and Kim are witnessing is potentially one of their first disputes in relationships? Conflicts of relationships exist in all relationships since it is almost impossible for two individuals to see something from the very same viewpoint. Conflicts in relationships need not always be perceived in a negative light, though. Conflict can also bring people back together if treated properly. Let's look at some of the key problems that cause the relationships to clash.

There are several different forms and sources of conflict. Some of the most popular ones include: children-it can be stressful business having babies! The tension between Kevin and Kim over their mixed family situation obviously isn't special. If you encourage them, children will wreak havoc on relationships. They need time and commitment, which can leave a feeling of a step-parent lonely and alone.

Finance-Money is one of the main triggers of relationship conflict. The beginning relationship problems will all be how you invest, earn, or budget money as a pair.

Personal Intimacy-When one partner's sexual desires vary from the other partner's; this may give rise to tension over relationships.

Insecurity-this may trigger disputes when one partner appears to feel insecure about their partnership and meaning to the other partner. Insecurity may also result in allegations of unfaithfulness.

Household Responsibilities-When one spouse contributes significantly more to caring for basic household chores and responsibilities; resentment may be created.

Lack of Effective Communication-This has the potential to create an atmosphere of persistent underlying conflict when there is no communication in relationships, or the only communication that takes place consists of yelling and arguing.

Relationship Conflict and Power

It is important to remember that relationship conflict is often the result of a differential of fundamental power or perceived disparity of power within the relationship. All this means is that one person in the relationship is dependent on the other person, for some reason, but the other person does not share that dependency. It generates a power Imbalance that gives control to the non-dependent partner, who can use the control over the other partner in a threatening way.

Let's assume, for example, Ann and Jeff were married for 18 years. They both had good careers before Ann unexpectedly decided to retire, even without Jeff's input. Jeff is resentful of this sudden turn of events while Ann finds herself entirely reliant on her husband financially. While their marriage has taken a downward turn, and Ann even thinks Jeff may have an affair, she is committed to making things work because she needs Jeff to keep her lifestyle going.

CONCLUSION

No relationship is sure, and that can be hard to acknowledge.

You will most likely be unable to altogether keep away from all relationship uneasiness. Yet, there are various things you could do to calm the steady addressing and invest more energy getting a charge out of what you have with your accomplice.

This report is designed to provide precise and solid information on the issue and issue secured. The supply is marketed with the alternative of not allowing the manufacturer to make book-keeping, officially approved administrations or anything else. If an exhortation is important, legitimate or competent, a rehearsed person in the call should be requested.

The Statement of Values, which was also accepted and approved by the American Bar Association Commission and the Publications & Associations Panel.

It is not permissible to replicate copy or transmit any part of this report in any electronic method or group. Authorization of this delivery is carefully disallowed, and the report's ability is not allowed unless the seller has written the approval. All ownership. All rights held.

The data provided herein is conveyed, to be truthful and consistent in that the beneficiary's clear and articulate duty is any danger, in so far as absence of attitude or otherwise, through any use or misuse of any methods, procedures or belongings inside them. Any legal obligation or liability will be kept against the seller for any reparation, damage or financial misfortune because of the results, either clearly or inferred.

All copyrights not held by the distributor are claimed by particular creators.

The statistics in this paper are primarily for educational purposes and are all-inclusive. The data are entered without a contract or any confirmation of assurance.

The trademarks used are without consent and the trademark distribution is without the consent or support of the trademark owner. Both trademarks and trademarks in the book are solely for the purpose of illustrating and are clearly managed and not associated by the founders.

CPSIA information can be obtained
at www.ICGtesting.com
Printed in the USA
BVHW091917220621
610211BV00006B/1773

9 781803 344584